HIDDEN TREASURES

SOUTH LANARKSHIRE

Edited by Simon Harwin

First published in Great Britain in 2002 by
YOUNG WRITERS
Remus House,
Coltsfoot Drive,
Peterborough, PE2 9JX
Telephone (01733) 890066

HB ISBN 0 75433 954 8
SB ISBN 0 75433 955 6

FOREWORD

This year, the Young Writers' Hidden Treasures competition proudly presents a showcase of the best poetic talent from over 72,000 up-and-coming writers nationwide.

Young Writers was established in 1991 and we are still successful, even in today's technologically-led world, in promoting and encouraging the reading and writing of poetry.

The thought, effort, imagination and hard work put into each poem impressed us all, and once again, the task of selecting poems was a difficult one, but nevertheless, an enjoyable experience.

We hope you are as pleased as we are with the final selection and that you and your family continue to be entertained with *Hidden Treasures South Lanarkshire* for many years to come.

CONTENTS

Louise Hutton	18
Jamie Hart	18
Neil McEwen	18
Christopher Falconer	19
Christopher Currie	19
Stacy McMillan	20
Heather Simmons	20
Darren Walter	21
Nicolle Drummond	21
Kayleigh Drummond	22
James Honeyman	22
Lauren Kennedy	23
Emma Hart	23
Kayleigh Reid	24
Deborah Muir	24
Martin Scott	25
Kendell Gallagher	25
Kerry Butchart	26
Daniel Walter	26
Rebecca Cowie	27
Hayley Rae	27
Sarah-Jane Siberry	28
Louise Hendry	28
Craig Williamson	29
Gemma McClarence	29
Amanda Burrowes	30
Gemma Brown	30
Megan Ross	30
Darren Smith	31
Lauren McAllister	31
Claire Gilmour	32
Louise Brown	32
Marie Claire Chalmers	33

Chatelherault Primary School

Rona Lees	33
Alison McLean	34
Alasdair Wilson	34

Greg Barclay	57
Dawn McConnell	57

David Livingstone Memorial Primary School

Jennifer Neil	58
Andrew Cox	58
Euan Ronaldson	59
Kirsten Darling	60
Lisa Rodmell	60
Lauren Munro	61
Ryan Whyte	62
Nicola Rennie	62
Stuart Thom	63
Amanda Burns	63
Lindsay Jane Murdoch	64
Kirsty Robertson	64
Carly McPhee	65
Ashleigh Larkin	65
Nicola McPadden	66
Suzanne Traynor	66
Lauren McKenzie	67
Cody Codona	67
Erin Dean	68
Liam McMillan	68
Aimee Irvine	69
Steven Reid	69
Erin Kelly	70
Kayleigh Hughes	70
Sarah Gormley	71
Robert Gracie	71

Glassford Primary School

Martin Grove	72
Stephanie Donaldson	72
Ross Clacher	72
Lorna Johnston	73
Scott Kemp	73
Stephanie Speedie	74

Rebekah Tait	74
Laura McNiven	75
Allison Marshall	75
Gillian Crozier	76
Alan Dawson	76
Louise Fleming	77
Nicholas Smith	77
Calum Johnston	78
Jack Fleming	78
Nikki Andrews	79
Caroline Marshall	79

High Blantyre Primary School

Charlotte Walton	80
Emma Aitken	80
Ian Robertson	80
Julie Boles	81
James Taylor	81
Jody Flannigan	82
Mark McQueeney	82
Graham Russell	83
Ryan McDonald	83
Karen Young	84
Ryan Kelly	84
Lisa Ireland	85
Andrew Henderson	85
Carly Taylor	86
Christopher Lyon	86
Ashley Pryce	87
Jordan Tennant	87

Lanark Primary School

Steven Smith	88
Victoria Wilson	88
Aimee Howland	89
Lauren Cosgrove	90
Steven Flynn	90
Cara McAlindin	91

Wionna Fox	92
Amy Gallacher	92
Zoe Prentice	93
Lee Robb	93
Fiona Scott	93
Fraser Campbell	94
Emma Robertson	94
Linzi Foster	95
Ronan Turner	95
Katie McGaan	96
Ruaraidh Gardner	96
Darryl Cavers	97
Michael Coyle	97
Gavin Alston	98
Jennifer Lang	98
Stewart Bell	99

Long Calderwood Primary School

Robert Phillips	99
Lorna MacPherson	100
Lisa McGraw	100
Catriona Murray	101
Luke Pryce	101
Callum MacDougall	102
Sacha Louise Brammer	102
George Lawton	103
Danielle Mitchell	103
Stephanie Alexander	104
April Rankin	104
Paula Copeland	105
Jamie Collins	105
Sheryl McFarlane	106
Nicole Hamilton	106
Caitlin Grace	107
Chris MacDonald	107
Rebecca Young	108
Gemma Stewart	108

Murray Primary School

Mark McQueenie	108
Nicola Gillan	109
Nicole Gibson	109
Marc Thomson	110
Claire Hastings	110
Graeme Smith	111
Libby Hoban	111
Rachel Steel	112
Colin Greeves	112
Michael Kent	113
Lorna Kyle	113
David Woodhouse	114
Graeme Bogle	114
Susan Gardiner	115
Kayleigh Hill	115
Alyesha McEwan	116
Sean Massie	116
Catriona Meechan	117
Jennifer Crawford	117
Eleanor Turner	118
Stevan Harris	118
Emma Wilkie	119
Sean Swindells-Dallas	120

Newfield Primary School

Kelly Jackson	120
Gillian Lambie	121
Shahla Mirbakhtiar	121
Kimberley Walker	122
Liam Thomson	122
Steven Forrest	122
Laura Thomson	123
Catriona Harkness	123
Adele Mitchell	124
Graeme Lindsay	124
Graeme Copland	125
Laura Hinshelwood	125

The Poems

HIDDEN GOLD

In a cool dark place where nobody goes,
There's a big, black field,
Where it's scary to go.

I was digging and digging,
Then I hit something hard
And do you know what it was?
My Crunchies and gold
That I hid there yesterday
And nobody told.

Sean Park (10)

TIGER'S SORROW

I was once a proud and beautiful tiger roaming through the jungle,
The most feared animal of all,
But then one day I went a-hunting only to find that I was the hunted.
Creeping through the long, dry grass I lunged at a young antelope,
Just then a terrifying noise filled the air
And as the sky exploded, I felt a sharp stab of pain,
Everything went black.
When I awoke from my deep sleep,
It was only to find myself in a very different place.
Instead of the lovely clean water of the waterhole,
There was a deep ravine.
I looked at it disgusted and then I looked beyond it.
Menacing steel bars, stronger even than the great gorilla.
I'm sure I have seen them before, once, in a nightmare.
But worse still beyond them, are the creatures who haunt my dreams,
They stare, they laugh, they shout and point,
I long to pounce and roar and bite,
But the deep muddy ditch cannot be crossed,
It protects them like a moat protects a castle.
I growl and enter my dark rocky cave,
Then, much later when I emerge from the darkness,
My eyes wander to the prison next to mine,
Where monkeys screech and yell and swing,
Then to the other where giraffes rustle leaves.
There is no hope of sleep tonight.

Laura Clark (11)
Blackwood Primary School

HIDDEN TREASURE

Hidden treasure under the sea,
I just wonder where it can be?
I looked under the sea,
It is nowhere to be seen,

I have checked on the sand,
Nobody knows where it can be.
Suddenly I saw the treasure
And I was filled with great pleasure.

Kayleigh Brownlie (9)
Carnwath Primary School

HIDDEN TREASURE

I was playing hide-and-seek,
When I hid in a small gap,
I found an old, ripped treasure map,
What a clever me!
Precious games, valuable rubies, shiny gold, hidden deep,
'Where?' says me.
Then I see,
Deep, deep down in the sea.
'How do I get it?' says me,
It says there is a secret key
In an old pirate shipwreck,
In the deep blue sea.
Then I swam to the bottom of the sea,
There were lots of fish swimming deep.
I found the secret key,
I swam a bit further,
Then I saw,
A great big treasure chest!
I had to swim a bit deeper,
Then I unlocked the treasure chest,
It glittered and shone and belonged to me.

Stephanie McVie (10)
Carnwath Primary School

THE HIDDEN TREASURE

I looked high,
I looked low.
I just didn't know
Which place to go.
On top of the fridge,
Down by the door,
On the table,
On the floor.
To the left
Or to the right,
Which way shall
I go tonight?
Then I see someone
Swimming in the river,
However, then I see it,
Sparkling, gold.
A treasure
Never to be sold.

Jennifer Arthur (10)
Carnwath Primary School

HIDDEN TREASURE

Hidden treasure, oh where could it be?
Under the shipwreck, inside the cave?
Beside the octopus?
Hidden treasure, oh where could you be?
I searched high,
I searched low, but I didn't know where to go.

4

I found the map that gave me a clue,
But I still didn't know what to do.
Go after the treasure?
Go home for my tea?
Hidden treasure, oh where could you be?

Stuart Dickson (10)
Carnwath Primary School

HIDDEN TREASURE

The hidden treasure, where could it be?
It's not in my bedroom and it's not near me.
I have looked everywhere,
Even beside the teddy bear.

I have looked in every cupboard in my house,
But all I've found is a little mouse.
I've looked in the garden and under the stairs,
But all I can find are more teddy bears.

I've looked in my classroom, my dad's car too,
I couldn't find it and neither could you.
I've looked under my covers, but it's not there,
I will never find it but that's not fair!

I've looked under the books and over the wall,
But I could not find it at all.
I've looked at my gran's and my auntie's as well,
I even looked down the old, old well.

I've looked up in the attic and under the ground,
But where is this treasure really to be found?
The hidden treasure, where could it be?
I know, it's under the sea!

Daniel Munro (10)
Carnwath Primary School

PIRATE TREASURE

One day while I was diving
where seaweed and plants were growing
fish and seals appeared to be
playing hide-and-seek.
I caught a glimmer from
the corner of my eye,
something shining from
the light of the sky.
It moved so silky smooth
as it coasted through the water
and quickly disappeared behind a coral cluster.
I swam around the coral and then to my surprise
I saw a pirate shipwreck right before my eyes.
As I swam much closer,
gleaming in the sand
was all the pirate treasure,
scattered all around.
Gold and jewels and things
lay sparkling in the sunlight,
just like all the stars in the sky at night.
I knew I had to leave the treasure
because it wasn't mine to take,
but it would have been nice
to have just one wee piece,
as a little souvenir
of swimming in the deep.

Hayley Carmichael (9)
Carnwath Primary School

HIDDEN TREASURE

My hidden treasure is not made of gold or filled with pretty jewels,
She is beautiful and priceless.
Her name is Isis.
She cuddles me when I am sad
And makes me laugh when she is bad.

She purrs at me and makes me happy,
She is my little green-eyed catty.
She wears a collar that has a bell,
That jingles all day from April to May.

If I ever lost her, I would search for miles,
Even though I know she has nine lives.
She is cuddly and sweet, my hidden treasure,
My cat, Isis.

Shelley Paul (10)
Carnwath Primary School

HIDDEN TREASURE

Once there was some hidden treasure that nobody could find,
I had a look under my bed, behind the cooker, in my shed.
I looked for hours and hours.
Then I went scuba-diving with my dad,
We went two miles deep,
Then I saw a little gap in a mountain.
I was small enough to get through.
Then I saw it, a huge and big bag with a dollar sign on it.
I opened the bag and there it was.

Ross Brown (10)
Carnwath Primary School

HIDDEN TREASURE

I looked in the garden,
I looked in the house,
I looked everywhere,
But no treasure was found.
I looked in the kitchen,
Bathroom and hall,
The treasure was nowhere,
Nowhere at all.
I looked in the shed and under the bed,
I looked in the cupboard,
Then I discovered,
I thought of the attic.
I knew what to do,
I climbed up a ladder,
Then I saw a key,
I took it, I went to my room.

Kirsty White (10)
Carnwath Primary School

HIDDEN TREASURE

I once found treasure at the bottom of the sea,
I took it up with a flea.
Then one day it went wee.
I hid it from everyone, just in case,
The flea got eaten by the frog.
It was very precious to me because it was diamonds,
Rubies, gold and silver.
Lots of precious things for me
And the flea, ha, ha!

Gemma Malone (9)
Carnwath Primary School

OH TREASURE

Hidden treasure to be found,
Not always underground.
Treasure is gold,
You must unfold.

What will I find?
Oh I wonder,
It might be kind!

I lift the lid, what will I find?
Warm thoughts rush
Through my mind.

I put my hand in to see if it glows
And pulled it out
As it is
A golden rose!

Kelly Kirkhope (10)
Carnwath Primary School

HIDDEN TREASURE

I looked high, I looked low
I just did not know where to go
I climbed the hills, I swam so deep
I just did not know
Then I saw down below
Hidden treasure
On the shore.

Katrina Sommerville (10)
Carnwath Primary School

HIDDEN TREASURE

Hidden treasure, where could it be?
In the cupboard or in the tree?
I just can't seem to find the treasure;
My brother puts me under too much pressure.
I looked at the beach but still there was no treasure.
I looked everywhere high and low and then I saw a tiny glow.
I went around beach to beach
And I suddenly saw an enormous glow.
There it was, it was the glow.
I followed the glow and the treasure
Was lying at the bottom of the sea.

Scott Semple (10)
Carnwath Primary School

TREASURE!

The sea is big and greeny-blue,
That all the fish swim through,
Deep, deep below among lots of fish,
Is something only I could wish.
It's surrounded and guarded by massive fish,
It's the largest treasure chest I could ever wish.
As it opens you're dazzled by the sparkly light,
All multicoloured and very bright,
Pearls and jewels galore,
Who could ask for anymore?

Robert Whitelaw (10)
Carnwath Primary School

HIDDEN TREASURE

Where can I find this treasure? It is not anywhere.
I have searched every place, but I can't find a trace.
I searched on the bed, under it, I searched the beach,
It wasn't there.
This led me to one place.
I searched the sea, sea caves too and some shipwrecks,
But it was not there.
Then I searched the house,
It was there I found it, under the table.
Sparkling, glowing, a box glowing gold.
Now I've found the treasure!

Calum Graham (10)
Carnwath Primary School

HIDDEN TREASURE

Secret treasure hidden deep
All the better for me to keep
Maybe in a hole or maybe in a ditch
So when I find it, I'll be rich

When I find it, it'll be hard to disguise
Lying there in front of my eyes
Where shall I hide it, in the cupboard, behind the door?
I'm certainly not leaving it on the floor.

Maybe it's new or maybe it's old,
But this hidden treasure is never to be sold.

Ruari Douglas (10)
Carnwath Primary School

HIDDEN TREASURE

On a cliff I did walk,
Saw some steps so did a trot,
To the bottom I did go.
Walking through the sand I saw,
I was amazed, it was a cave,
Full of items, old and gold,
Worth a fortune I was told.
I thought, should I tell?
No one would care.
I looked high and low,
No one was there,
Except the waves.
Is there more I thought? Yes,
At the back,
No, better not go.

Ashley Imrie (10)
Carnwath Primary School

HIDDEN TREASURE

There's some treasure at the bottom of the sea,
For me, all gold and silver,
It's been waiting for me for years and years
And soon I am going to find it.
If I find it and it's not gold,
I will just keep looking for my hidden treasure.

Mandy Kerr (10)
Carnwath Primary School

HIDDEN TREASURE

Where can I find this treasure?
I've searched top to bottom and still can't find it.
I wonder where it could be?
Then I thought of a place it could be in,
I thought it could be at the beach, but then I thought no.
So I asked my mum and dad, 'Where can I find treasure?'
And they said, 'In an obvious place'
And it came to me, in the sea.
So we went there, but it wasn't there.
I was still wondering where it could be,
When I saw my dog dig something out of the garden,
I went over and my dog had found the hidden treasure!

Richard McLelland (10)
Carnwath Primary School

HIDDEN TREASURE

Is it in the living room
Or behind the chair?
Oh dear, oh dear, where could it be?
Maybe it is in my bedroom
Or under my bed?
In my drawers?
Under the desks?
Oh there it is,
My teddy bear called Tom.

Claire Forsyth (9)
Carnwath Primary School

HIDDEN TREASURE

I looked high, I looked low,
I just gave a sigh for walking so slow,
I looked up, I looked down, to find a chest full of pleasure,
Then I saw something sparkle, but it was just a sparkly bottle.

Suddenly I saw a gap and inside it was a map,
It showed a picture of a tree with the cool blue sea,
It told me to look in the north-east,
But I could not go there because it's so deep.

Suddenly I found the treasure,
Inside was some gold, silver, bronze
And lots and lots of coins,
Now I am so happy that I found the hidden treasure.

Ann Robertson (10)
Carnwath Primary School

HIDDEN TREASURE

Once there was some treasure buried under the seabed,
I had a look for it under the bed,
Behind the cooker, nearly everywhere,
But no luck.
I went to ask my mum and dad,
They said most treasure was under the sea.
I went to have a look, it wasn't there.
Then it came to me, it was in my friend's house!
He said he had a treasure set in his room.
I went over to his house, there it was,
My quest was over!

William Smart (10)
Carnwath Primary School

MY HIDDEN TREASURE

I looked high,
I looked low,
I just gave a sigh,
Because I was slow.

I thought I would go home,
I walked by myself, all alone,
All of a sudden, I saw a sack,
I picked it up and heard a crack.

I thought it would be the hidden treasure,
But it wasn't to my displeasure,
It wasn't the hidden gold,
It was some fruit, covered in mould.

I also found some stumps and a broken wicket,
Which are used for a game of cricket.
So I kept walking further on,
Until I came to the ocean.
It felt like I had swallowed a potion,
I looked down, I thought I was imagining things,
Then I saw some fancy rings.

So I went to check it out and go for a swim,
I swam around and it looked quite dim,
I looked below and saw something shiny,
I swam to it and it was tiny.

All of a sudden I was filled with pleasure,
I saw a chest filled with treasure,
It was covered in seaweed, but I didn't care,
I opened the chest and started to stare,
Gold, silver, jewels and gems shining bright,
Sparkling like the stars on a frosty night!

Danielle Steele (10)
Carnwath Primary School

MY LITTLE BROTHER

My little brother is cute
My little brother is kind
He is helpful and he is caring
When I am upset we play together
And have lots of fun
He shares his toys with me and is lovely
I love him and he loves me
But sometimes, oh sometimes he's soooo mean and nasty
But I still love him, my little brother.

Ashley Whitton (9)
Cathkin Primary School

MY BEST FRIEND

We do everything together,
We have fun, lots of fun.
It is excellent,
We go to play football on the pitches.
We go to the shops,
He stays overnight,
I love to play with my best friend.

David Brock (9)
Cathkin Primary School

IF I RULED THE WORLD

If I ruled the world
I would make it that people would stop fighting over silly things
I would make it that you could stop animals getting killed over
Foot-and-mouth disease

And stop arguments happening
I would cure all the diseases in the world
Help people to get homes when floods come
And forgive people when they fall out.

Lauren Purdie (11)
Cathkin Primary School

MY BIRTHDAY

I like my birthday because it's fun
My brother comes to my gran and granpa's
I have a party and get lots of presents

I open my presents
Say 'Yes!' to my bike
Thank you Mum and Dad
I love my birthday.

Mark McCutcheon (9)
Cathkin Primary School

MY BEST FRIEND

My best friend is Belinda, because she is so kind
We play together nearly all the time

My best friend is Belinda, we've always been friends
We always climb trees and we like to make dens

My best friend is Belinda, we always go to church
I see her every day cos I like her very much.

Amy Moffat (9)
Cathkin Primary School

EASTER TIME IS HERE

Easter time is here, everybody cheer
Stuffing their faces with chocolate
Mmm, I like chocolate
Easter bunny comes at night
He gives us chocolate and says, 'Night, night'
I like chocolate, it's so good
I like chocolate, it's my favourite food
I'm a chocoholic
Easter time is here, everybody cheer!

Louise Hutton (9)
Cathkin Primary School

MY BEST FRIEND

My best friends are always around
When I am sick, when I am on holiday
I think of them all the time

When I am at the shops, I buy them sweets
Even if they are not there
They are always on my mind.

Jamie Hart (9)
Cathkin Primary School

MY BIRTHDAY

I woke up, it was a sunny day,
I said, 'Why can't I go out to play?'
Mum said, 'Because you have school today.'
I said, 'But it's my birthday.'

I opened my presents,
Wow, what a great day,
After that I went out to play,
Then I had a perfect day.

Neil McEwen (9)
Cathkin Primary School

CHRISTMAS TIME

Christmas is near
Santa is near
Snowflakes are falling
Best friends are calling
Santa is delivering presents
Everyone wakes and runs down the stairs
To open their presents
Then Christmas is over.

Christopher Falconer (9)
Cathkin Primary School

IF I RULED THE WORLD

If I ruled the world
I would make peace among mankind
So everyone will be safe
And we are happy all the time
So people will be kind to each other
I would stop the terrorism in America
And everyone will live in peace
I would try to cure all diseases
To stop people dying at young and old ages.

Christopher Currie (11)
Cathkin Primary School

IF I RULED THE WORLD

If I ruled the world
I would share my money
With the people in need
And there would be lots of happy faces

If I ruled the world
My family's birthdays
Would be the happiest days of their lives
There would be joy on their faces

If I ruled the world
There would be more police
And plenty of peace

If I ruled the world
I would run to the shops
And buy chocolate
And school would finish at 10 o'clock.

Stacy McMillan (8)
Cathkin Primary School

HIDDEN TREASURE

Under the sea,
Surrounded by mermaids and fish
And a starfish as well,
A little, wooden chest lives there,
Holding gold, rubies, rings and other things too.
Where has it come from?
Pirates could have stolen it,
I wonder?

Heather Simmons (8)
Cathkin Primary School

IF I RULED THE WORLD

If I ruled the world
All the fights would stop
And we would not argue

If I ruled the world
All the families would love each other
Instead of fighting and arguing

If I ruled the world
There would be peace outside
For people to play in

If I ruled the world
I would have all the cats in the whole wide world
And have all the chocolate spread.

Darren Walter (8)
Cathkin Primary School

HIDDEN TREASURE

Under the sea,
I can see my treasure,
With tiger sharks swimming all around it,
On a big, sunken ship,
Tangled with seaweed,
A rusty, wooden treasure chest,
It holds silver and gold,
Tiaras and jewellery, coins too.
Where has it come from?
Pirates have sunk it to the bottom,
With the King and his royal family.

Nicolle Drummond (8)
Cathkin Primary School

IF I RULED THE WORLD

If I ruled the world
I would bring peace
And joy to all of the people in America
And all of the other people at war
And I would give money to all of the poor orphans

If I ruled the world
I would make sure that every family has food and water
And if it was their birthday
I would make it the best day of their life

If I ruled the world
I would take care of my little brother and sister
And I would start eating healthy food

If I ruled the world
I would make all of the head teachers
Let us go out to play for two extra hours.

Kayleigh Drummond (8)
Cathkin Primary School

HIDDEN TREASURE

Under the sea,
In a sunken ship,
Surrounded by electric eels and crabs,
A carved, wooden treasure chest,
Holds gems, gold coins and crowns.
Where has it come from?
Pirates have stolen it from ships.

James Honeyman (8)
Cathkin Primary School

IF I RULED THE WORLD

If I ruled the world
I would give money to children in need
And to the people in America

If I ruled the world
Families would not fight
Or do anything bad

If I ruled the world
I'd make the world safe
And see happy faces

If I ruled the world
School would finish at 9.30am!

Lauren Kennedy (7)
Cathkin Primary School

HIDDEN TREASURE

Under the sea,
In a sunken ship,
Covered with leeches, electric eels and even seahorses,
They were vicious and cruel.
It's a gold and rusty treasure chest,
Holding crowns, keys, rubies, diamonds and tiaras.
Where had it come from?
Pirates had stolen it from the palace,
The king was furious, so he sent guards,
But they did not find it, ever.

Emma Hart (8)
Cathkin Primary School

IF I RULED THE WORLD

If I ruled the world
I would give food
And hundreds of pounds
To children in need
And food to children in Africa

If I ruled the world
When it was my family's birthdays
I would make it the happiest day of their lives
And give them hundreds of presents

If I ruled the world
I would be safe from wars
And nobody would get killed

If I ruled the world
Schools would not be built
And I would eat lots of chocolate!

Kayleigh Reid (8)
Cathkin Primary School

HIDDEN TREASURE

Under the sea,
Tangled in seaweed,
On the seabed,
There is a gold and diamond
Treasure chest,
It holds jewels and diamond tiaras.
Where has it come from?
It was stolen from the ships.

Deborah Muir (8)
Cathkin Primary School

IF I RULED THE WORLD

If I ruled the world
There would be food for everyone
And no murders

If I ruled the world
Families would show respect
And love and wouldn't fight

If I ruled the world
I'd make the world a safer place
And I'd play all day

If I ruled the world
In school there would be
Writing poems all day.

Martin Scott (8)
Cathkin Primary School

HIDDEN TREASURE

Down in the dark blue sea,
Where the dolphins sleep,
Big, purple octopuses in the blue sea,
But down in the seaweed,
There's something rusty, maybe it's a chest?
It holds things that I dream of,
Like rubies and blue sapphires,
With lots more.
Where has it come from?
I wonder if pirates have lowered
Down the treasure with an anchor?

Kendell Gallagher (7)
Cathkin Primary School

A SCOTTISH GALE

The other day the high winds struck,
Toppling trees and the odd truck.
Power lines came down, so no more electric,
Around the city the traffic was hectic.
Some buses were cancelled and even some trains,
I really don't envy the weather vanes.
From the roofs came slates and tiles,
The winds caused destruction for miles and miles.
They closed the Kingston and the Erskine bridges,
I'm glad I wasn't on any high ridges.
Along the coast, waves battered the shore,
I'm glad I'm safe behind my door.

Kerry Butchart (10)
Cathkin Primary School

IF I RULED THE WORLD

If I ruled the world, I would sail the seven seas.
If I ruled the world, I would build my mum a better house.

If I ruled the world, I would help the poor and give them homes.
If I ruled the world, I would help the school onto the internet.

If I ruled the world, I would help Third World countries.
If I ruled the world, I would help world peace
By taking all the guns away in the world.

If I ruled the world . . .

Daniel Walter (9)
Cathkin Primary School

CHRISTMAS

Christmas is here
Hip hip hooray
Santa is near
Children cheer
Snowflakes are falling
Children are calling

Santa is here
Hip hip hooray
Children are cheering
Into the living room we go
Open our presents, one by one
Got a new bike, yes!

Santa has gone
Children are sad
Until next year
Goodbye Santa.

Rebecca Cowie (9)
Cathkin Primary School

IF I RULED THE WORLD

If I ruled the world
I would give help to sick people
If I ruled the world
I would buy my big sister a new dress
And help her look her best
If I ruled the world
I would eat all the chocolate in the world.

Hayley Rae (7)
Cathkin Primary School

MY BIG SISTER

My big sister is helpful and kind,
Loving, hugging, sharing and caring,
She also looks nice, lovely in fact,
She cares for me and plays with me,
She makes me tea and toast,
She loves me, I love her,
That's what matters most.

My big sister is nasty and mean,
She sometimes gets on my nerves,
She blames things on me,
But after all, we are sisters,
I love her, she loves me
And that's what matters most.

Sarah-Jane Siberry (9)
Cathkin Primary School

IF I RULED THE WORLD

If I ruled the world
I would make it that people
Who start terrible things like terrorism,
Fighting and all the other bad things, stop
I would make it that the people
Who start it, would not get punished
I would make it all stop
Before any more people get hurt
I would help the people in America
And help in any way I could
I would bring happiness for them.

Louise Hendry (10)
Cathkin Primary School

IF I RULED THE WORLD

If I ruled the world I would make it a much better place
So people would get along and like each other
I would make it that everyone would laugh and have friends
I would make it that the terrorism would stop
And we must always work together
Then this world would be a better place for anyone
Even the animals
In Pakistan and in Belfast the arguments would stop too
Bullying, floods and foot-and-mouth
Are disasters for everyone in the world
I would make it all stop.

Craig Williamson (11)
Cathkin Primary School

WINTERTIME

Winter is here, Christmas is near
Snowflakes are falling, best friends are calling
I am wrapped up in my cosy coat, playing at snowball fights

Turkey is in the oven, waiting for my tea
When will it be ready? I'm very hungry!

Then I hang up my stocking and climb the stairs
I jump into my bed and say my prayers

Then I wake up, run down the stairs
My presents are there, yippee!

Gemma McClarence (8)
Cathkin Primary School

My Best Friend

My best friend is Gemma,
We stay with each other,
We go to the shops, we go to my gran's,
We go to the beach, we play on the sand,
I love my best friend very much.

Amanda Burrowes (9)
Cathkin Primary School

Summertime

In the summertime,
Water is splashing, children are playing,
Flowers are glowing, the wind isn't blowing,
People are happy, good times all the way,
I wish it was summer every day.

Gemma Brown (9)
Cathkin Primary School

Spring

I can see all the flowers appearing
And lambs are born
Spring brings new life and hope
I love spring a lot
It brings heat to the cool winter air.

Megan Ross (9)
Cathkin Primary School

IF I RULED THE WORLD

If I ruled the world
I would make it that one day all the terrorism
In some parts of the country
And all the fighting in the world would stop
And I would make it that people with different coloured skin
And religion, would come together with peace and enjoyment
And would live in a better and happier world
I would make all the bullying stop
And people would sit down and talk about
Why people were doing it
So you could make friends with the person
And play happily.

Darren Smith (11)
Cathkin Primary School

IF I RULED THE WORLD

If I ruled the world, I would make it that
I would not argue with my big brother
I would stop getting into bother
I would make all the fights and wars end
And everybody would be friends
I would make everybody come together
I would make world peace last forever
I would make illnesses stop spreading
And people stop dying
I would stop everyone from fighting
Because it leads to terrible wars.

Lauren McAllister (11)
Cathkin Primary School

IF I RULED THE WORLD

If I ruled the world
People would get on with each other and not fight
And I would keep the animals safe
All of the floods everywhere were bad
I would like to help the people who suffered in them
I would like to prevent what happened in America
From happening again
Lots of people have an illness
I would make them better
I would make people get happier soon.

Claire Gilmour (11)
Cathkin Primary School

STORM IN JANUARY 2002

Wind howling, fences smashing
Cars crashing, trees bashing
People windswept all over the place
Rain lashing down all over their face
Flooded in Helensburgh
Scaffolding poles fell in Edinburgh
Lucky escapes all over the place
My dad's van was saved from a watery grave
Worst storm since we were born
Let's hope it's nicer tomorrow morn.

Louise Brown (10)
Cathkin Primary School

IF I RULED THE WORLD

If I ruled the world
I would make it that we would all be happy
And would forgive each other.
All the poor people would have all the fun and games
Like everybody else.
We would all be treated the same
All the shops' prices would come all the way down to under a pound.
Everybody would love animals and not hate them.
Everybody would get their wishes if they really deserved them
And everybody would be loved.

Marie Claire Chalmers (11)
Cathkin Primary School

RONA'S PAINTBOX

Orange is the second colour of the beautiful rainbow,
Or it might be the fire flowing up into the sky on a cold winter night,
The fruit that tastes nice on a summer's day.

Blue is the colour of the waves at sea being tossed about by the wind,
It's also the colour of the great blue shark
And the planet Neptune floating high in space.

Yellow is the sun, dancing on the pool surface,
It's also the lights shining brightly on a dark, cold night
Or bananas dangling from a tree.

White is the snowmen I build on Christmas Day,
It might even be the fur on a nice, cuddly snow tiger
Or spooky ghosts haunting you.

Rona Lees (9)
Chatelherault Primary School

FOUR MAGIC SEASONS

Easter time is here, holidays drawing near
Chocolate is freshly made just for us to eat
All the flowers spring up for us to meet

Sunshine shines in the sky
The holiday season's drawing near
The children are happy as you can see
The bees are near the honey tree

Fireworks are blazing high
The wind is blowing in the sky
The leaves are falling on the ground
Spooky Hallowe'en is coming round

The snow is here
Christmas time is near
Our festive spirits are growing
Our Christmas turkeys are cooking
Santa Claus is near
For Christmas time is here.

Alison McLean (11)
Chatelherault Primary School

THE STORY OF THE SEASONS

Springtime babies,
Jumping with joy,
Spring is near,
Did you hear?

Summer is hot,
Go and play,
Not doing bad things,
But playing games.

Autumn is windy,
Leaves are falling,
Flowers are hiding,
Don't get upset, it's autumn time.

Winter, winter, we like winter,
Winter is snowy, it is cold,
But children like it because
Santa's coming.

Alasdair Wilson (11)
Chatelherault Primary School

WHAT SEASONS MEAN TO ME

Autumn time is cold and wet when you go out
Trick or treating, make sure you wrap up tight
Watch all the beautiful colours as you light your fireworks
And remember Guy Fawkes is out

Springtime is here, the shops are full of Easter eggs
You just can't wait until you get yours
You love going to the farms and seeing all the baby animals
And remember to play some tricks on your friends, because it's April
Fool's Day

Summer is here, grab your sun hat and suncream and head to the beach
Go swimming in the pool, that will cool you off
But don't enjoy yourself too much
Because you still have to go back to school

Hooray, winter is here, get outside and build your snowman
Remember, don't throw your snowballs too hard
Because you could hurt someone
Get your hat and gloves because it's going to be a cold season.

Marnie Nicol (11)
Chatelherault Primary School

ALL AROUND THE YEAR

Easter bunny bouncing around
Hiding eggs from your tummy
New animals are jumping around
Because new life is born today

Beef burgers roast on the grill
For a nice barbecued meal
Bees and wasps sting little boys and girls
Water fights make a mess
But boys and girls find it fun

Leaves fall from the trees
As people in funny costumes
Go trick or treating
People stand round a big fire
With fireworks and sparklers

Snow falling from the sky
Snowballs fly and boys and girls make snowmen
Robins singing at Christmas time
Children and their father and mother
Sit around the Christmas tree
Opening their presents and having Christmas dinner.

Alexander Lowrie (11)
Chatelherault Primary School

BECKY'S PAINTBOX

Red is the colour of a bright red rose
Or the bright red apple on a big apple tree
Or lipstick on someone's lips.

The silver tears running down someone's face
Or the fifty pence coin in a fat purse
Or the rain falling from the sky.

Blue is the colour of the sky,
The sea, with lots of people swimming in it
Or the colour of our school uniform.

Gold is a pound coin in a hand,
The sand beside the cold water
Or the treasure in a huge chest.

Becky Murdoch (9)
Chatelherault Primary School

MY YEAR

Easter is here, a fresh new start,
Babies are born, farmers kept busy,
As they help the new life to get ready.
A cool wind blows as the flowers grow,
Come on, it's summer, let's go.

Summertime, school is out,
No time for anger, let's all scream and shout,
'Cos now it's time to go away on a lovely holiday
Sandy beaches, summer lollies and ice creams too,
Let's nip off to autumn, what's new?

Autumn's here, ghosts are near,
As we begin preparation to scare,
'Cos Hallowe'en's such an important date
Try not to scare your mum or your mate.

Winter is cold with snowflakes falling,
You can't go outside at all,
Staying inside, kids are shouting and bawling,
Waiting for Santa's coming,
Hogmanay, let's all be happy and gay,
Happy New Year, hooray!

Stewart Wright (11)
Chatelherault Primary School

THE FOUR SEASONS OF THE YEAR

Springtime is here
Easter time is drawing near
New baby lambs and chicks
April Fool's is soon here
There is a new life on the way

Summer is here
And we're out of school
It's sunny and warm
So let's go out to play
Soon it will be time to go back

Autumn is here
The leaves are falling
We're out of school for a week
It's warm and rainy
Remember to watch the fireworks on the 5th November

Winter is here
It's snowing outside
Santa Claus is on his way with his reindeer
We will have a nice Christmas and open our presents
Then we will start a new year.

Amy Lindsay (11)
Chatelherault Primary School

KATIE'S PAINTBOX

White is the cloud floating through the summer sky
Or the top of a mountain
The moon on a wizard's hat

Yellow is the colour of the bright, bright sun
Or the sand on a beach
Or could be a yellow banana

Green is the colour of a springtime leaf
The stem of a lovely red rose
The colour of a caterpillar munching his lunch

Blue is the sky on a hot summer's day
The fifth colour in the beautiful rainbow
Or the deep blue sea.

Katie Galbraith (9)
Chatelherault Primary School

SEASONS OF THE YEAR

Springtime is Easter time,
This is when the bunny comes out to play.
Let's go and see
If there are any chocolate eggs to be found.

Summertime is play time,
Hear all the children play.
Don't forget the ice cream van
Which drives around all day.

Autumn time is when all the leaves fall,
See all the fireworks
Shooting up in the air which are bright,
See the Catherine wheels spin round.

Wintertime is Christmas time,
Unwrap all your presents.
As the turkey cooks in the oven,
Sing some Christmas carols,
While the night flows by.

Lauren McLear (11)
Chatelherault Primary School

KAY'S PAINTBOX

Red is the first colour of the rainbow,
Is an apple on the tree
Or might be someone's favourite colour.

White is a pearl at the seaside,
As snow on a winter's day,
Ghosts on a dark night.

Gold, buried under our feet,
As the sun up in the sky,
Stars sparkle in the moonlight.

Silver stars in the night-sky glowing,
Is the ring you might get for your wedding,
Could be tears streaming down your face.

Kay Law (9)
Chatelherault Primary School

RAIN

I like the rain, I like the rain,
It's fun and wet,
But when the sun comes out,
It's no fun,
I like the rain, do you?
I like the rain because it gives life to flowers,
I like the rain, I like the rain,
It gives me life,
Then the sun comes out,
Clouds seem so grey,
Then a rainbow comes out, rain falls,
Then I am wet again.

Natasha Stone (9)
Chatelherault Primary School

THE FOUR SEASONS

Winter

Christmas is merry, let's drink sherry
Lots of presents
Under the tree
And they are all for *me!*
Christmas rush
Snow turns to slush
But then we retire
To under the spire

Summer

Summer is here
Let's drink beer
Cool drinks flowing
The grass needs mowing
Your mum is in a happy mood
So let's eat all the food

Autumn

Leaves are falling
Blackbirds are bawling
Hallowe'en is here
Ghosts, witches and wizards everywhere

Spring

Lambs and foals it can bring
Let us all sing
Flowers grow everywhere
Oh look at that little hare!
This lovely season is called spring.

David Jenkins (11)
Chatelherault Primary School

JACK'S PAINTBOX

Gold

Gold stars sparkling in the night sky
Someone's ring sparkling in the sunshine
Gold cars driving up and down the street

Blue

Blue is a deep and cool pool
Blue is the sky
Blue whales splashing on a sunny day

Green

Green grass blowing in the summer's breeze
Leaves fluttering from the trees in a gentle wind
Or green chalk writing on the blackboard

Red

Red roller coasters going up and down the red rails
Or the red-hot sun shining in the sky
Firemen trying to get a fire out.

Jack Neilan (9)
Chatelherault Primary School

EUAN'S PAINTBOX

Blue is the sea, angry and restless
Or the sky on a sunny day
Or the colour of our language jotters at school

Red is the colour of the Manchester United home strip
Or a flame burning on Guy Fawkes Night
Or a Ferrari zooming past you

Orange is the colour of a fruit
Or the sky on a summer's night
And the colour of my friend's hair

Yellow is the colour of my hair
Or the sun glaring down on you
And the colour of a fruit called a banana.

Euan McVee (9)
Chatelherault Primary School

JACQUELINE'S PAINTBOX

Red

Red is the colour of our lips
Or a yummy red apple
Or flames of a burning fire on a cold winter's night.

Black

Black is the colour of a dark, dark night,
A haunted house with scary ghosts
Or a growling bear in a cave.

Green

Green leaves fluttering in the wind on a breezy day
Or a slithering lizard through the grass.

Blue

Blue is the colour of the sky on a summer's day
Or a deep, deep sea on a wild day
Or one of my favourite colours in the rainbow.

Jacqueline Sharpe (9)
Chatelherault Primary School

THE STORY OF THE FOUR SEASONS OF THE YEAR

Springtime is here
And Easter is near,
Springtime is here,
Rabbits are near,
Jump with joy, spring is here.

Summer is hot,
Go out to play,
Don't do bad things, summer is here,
The scent of roses
And the sun on our skin.

Autumn is windy,
The flowers are hiding,
Leaves are falling
And rain is coming,
Don't get upset, autumn is nearly gone.

Winter, winter, the best season of the year,
Autumn has gone, winter is here,
It is snowing, children are playing,
Ready for Santa to come.

Amer Iqbal (10)
Chatelherault Primary School

HOLLIE'S PAINTBOX

Black could be a cat on the end of a witch's broom,
A bat flying silently through the night
Or a rat running through my room.

Yellow could be hidden treasure buried in a cave,
Some bright bananas hanging on a tree
Or the sun setting on a light night

Green is like the fresh spring grass
Leaves falling from a tree
Or a bush with prickly thorns

White is like sparkling icicles hanging on a branch,
A thin scary ghost that haunts me through the night
Or a little cat that runs in the light.

Hollie Russell (9)
Chatelherault Primary School

SUPER SEASONS

Spring brings Easter here,
The Easter bunny brings some eggs,
New baby animals grow some legs,
Daffodils sprout from the ground
And that's how spring was found.

Summer brings some fun
And children have some fun,
The smell of roses,
Fills everyone's noses.

Autumn leaves fall to the ground
And for animals, new homes are found,
All the plants retreat to the soil
And this is a season not to be spoiled.

In winter snowballs fly,
Then presents everyone has to buy,
Jack Frost appears on the scene
And lots of happy faces are seen.

Scott McNab (11)
Chatelherault Primary School

THE SEASONS FOR ME

Easter time is here again
The bunnies are bouncing around
Rolling eggs down a hill
And seeing if they can be found
Around this time, new life is seen
The flowers are starting to bloom
Trees are gaining leaves again
Oh . . . remember to spring clean your room!

Summer's a time for holidays
And lying on a beach
But remember not to have
Too many ice lollies each!
Boiling hot - the sun's become
And you are free from school
Shorts and T-shirts you will wear but
Don't try to look too cool!

Autumn means leaves falling down
And rain, rain, rain, rain
Kids go out on Hallowe'en
Down the streets and lanes
Fireworks on Guy Fawkes Night
Blue and green and red
But kids, don't get too near them
Or you could end up dead!

Winter - weather's colder
Jack Frost lets it snow
If you go out unprepared
Inside you'll quickly go
Christmas time means presents
And parties to attend
Let's just hope your relatives
Don't drive you round the bend!

Iain Stepek (11)
Chatelherault Primary School

MAGIC SEASONS

Spring comes with Easter time,
All the chocolates will be mine,
The leaves grow with vines,
Babies arrive with a lot of joy.

When summer is here the weather is sunny,
Children in shorts and T-shirts having picnics,
Joyfully out of school and in the pool.

Guy Fawkes day in autumn,
Hallowe'en is coming, children make their costumes,
Leaves falling gently from the trees,
Dying insects like wasps and bees.

Children singing Christmas carols in the winter,
Unwrapping presents with wonder,
Snow slipping off the roof
And people making snowmen.

Christopher Cheung (11)
Chatelherault Primary School

STEVEN'S PAINTBOX

Black is the dark sky in the middle of the night
Or the black coal trains that come past on the rail tracks,
Black's also the colour of the blackboard that the teacher is ready
to write on.

Green is the colour of the grass on a lovely summer's day
Or the colour of the rainforest, in the middle of the summer,
Leaves fluttering from trees in an easy summer's breeze.

Yellow is the colour of the sun in the middle of a summer's day,
Yellow is the colour of the flowers blossoming at the bottom
of my garden
Or the colour of the pencil that I sometimes write with.

White is the colour of the lovely winter snow
Or sometimes the frost swaying on the tips of the long grass
Or the fluffy clouds up above in the lovely blue sky.

Steven Crawford (10)
Chatelherault Primary School

DECLAN'S PAINTBOX

Gold

The sun as it slowly sets on the distant horizon,
the sand sparkling in the sunlight
or gold treasure glimmering in a cave.

Silver

Is the crown on the Queen's head,
jewels in a treasure room
or the wet tears from your face.

Green

Green are leaves fluttering from the trees in a gentle summer breeze,
the grass tickling my toes
or emerald eyes glowing in the darkness.

Declan Timlin (9)
Chatelherault Primary School

THE SEASONS OF THE YEAR

Summer is here with clear blue skies
The sunshine shines high above
Warm, sandy beaches and clear blue seas
The holiday time we love to see

The spring has begun
New lambs are born
Wet grass with dew and sunny showers
Flowers are growing
New chicks are born
This is what spring is about

Leaves are falling from the trees
Hallowe'en is plain to see
Children going from door to door
Saying funny jokes or laughing galore

Wintertime, with mistletoe and wine
Children singing Christmas rhymes
Presents waiting under the tree
Soon it'll be Christmas Day.

Lauren McKinlay (11)
Chatelherault Primary School

FRASER'S PAINTBOX

Gold is like a posh watch reflecting the light
The sand on a beach winking up at me through all the towels
                                        and umbrellas
Or coins in the light waiting to be spent

Red is the colour of a hot bristling fire shooting up into the night's sky
Or the colour of anger when someone is angry
Or maybe a red-hot piece of bacon sizzling in a frying pan

Blue is the colour of a lovely calm pool
Maybe the colour of the sky on a lovely hot day
Or the cold frost on a winter's day

Silver is my tear running from my face
Or the colour of a ten pence piece glittering in the light
Even a star in the night sky.

Fraser Porteous (10)
Chatelherault Primary School

THE FOUR SEASONS

Spring is here, the leaves start to grow
New life, calf and foal
Easter time, lots of eggs
April Fool's coming near

Summertime, *school is out!*
And everyone is going away
Time to swim and have some fun
End of summer, the new school year starts

Autumn time, the leaves fall
Hallowe'en, trick or treat
Guy Fawkes, big fireworks!
St Andrew's Day, Irn-Bru and shortbread

Wintertime, loads of snow
Christmas time, loads of presents
Big, juicy turkey
New Year's Day, big celebrations.

Gary Seaton (11)
Chatelherault Primary School

PAUL'S PAINTBOX

Red is the colour of a ruby sparkling in the sun
Or a very juicy apple that's just been bitten in
Or blood streaming through your body keeping you alive

Yellow is the colour of the bright shining sun
Or the second colour in the rainbow which is a very bright one
Maybe even the colour of a butterfly fluttering away in the
bright yellow sun

White is the colour of a pearl, one of the ocean's jewels
Or snow falling on Christmas Day covering the streets in white
Or big, fluffy white clouds covering the sky

Green is the colour of the grass that cows like to eat
Or the colour of the pine trees that never lose their leaves
Or the colour of my sharpener sharpening my pencil.

Paul Toner (10)
Chatelherault Primary School

EWAN'S PAINTBOX

Red could be a thorny rose,
The colour of a clown's nose,
Red could be cherries, berries or a rosy apple.

Blue is the colour of a mountain stream,
Blue is the colour I see in my dream
Or the colour of mint ice cream

Black is a winged bat, a lurking cat
Black is the sky on a winter's night
A duelling fight, the Devil's kite
A monster waiting to pounce on his enemy

Silver is the colour of the moon
A couple exchanging silver rings
A statue's ears.

Ewan Kerr (10)
Chatelherault Primary School

ASHLEY'S PAINTBOX

Gold
Gold coins gleaming under the midnight sky
Or buried underground for miners to mine
Stars that sparkle in the glint of the moonlight

Red
Red is blood that travels through our bodies keeping us alive
Or roses, about to bloom on a new rose bush
Ripe apples, ready to fall and be eaten

Blue
Blue could be a pool in your back garden
Or a pen in my pencil case waiting for me to write with
As dark nights approach over our heads in winter

Orange
Orange is the sun burning miles away from the Earth
Or leaves fluttering down from the high trees
Burning fire on Bonfire Night all over the world.

Ashley Weir (9)
Chatelherault Primary School

DAVID'S PAINTBOX

White is the snow I wake up to on Christmas Day,
Could be frightening ghosts at Hallowe'en
And the teacher's chalk, ready to use every day on the blackboard.

Red is burning hot bonfires, bristling on Guy Fawkes Night
Or the planet Mars, seen through a telescope
And one of the colours on the Hamilton Accies football strip.

Orange is the sun slowly sinking down at night
Or the second colour of the rainbow
And one of the colours on the Irish flag.

Black is the pitch-black sky at night
Or the colour of charcoal used on my chess piece,
Is a mine where our coal comes from.

David Stewart (10)
Chatelherault Primary School

SEASONS OF LIFE

Spring

As Easter soon comes around
The Easter bunny hops about
He tries to find a place to hide
All the lovely Easter eggs

Summer

Hooray, it's summer and the sun is out
So why don't we sing and shout
We run around in our shorts and T-shirts
And then we jump into the swimming pool, *splash!*

Autumn

Hallowe'en has come
Everyone is looking for something to wear
Children prepare their song or joke
Trick or treating goes round the doors
Everyone comes home, glad and exhausted
Bags full of goodies now to eat

Winter

When my friends and I go out to play
We build a huge big snowman
We give him a scarf and a hat
And we try and make him look so much like my dad.

Melanie Clarke (11)
Chatelherault Primary School

THE DINOSAUR

A dinosaur peers round my bedroom door,
'Sleep tight' it shouts and waves a giant paw.
It roars and snores and settles on the floor,
But when I wake up, there's no dinosaur.

Beth Shearer, Jack Taylor, Emma Scullion, Heather McKie,
Emma Walker, Debbie McAdams (6), Gordon O'Neill,
Jamie McLakne & Andrew Stone (7)
Chatelherault Primary School

TEACHER SAYS ...

Teacher says - stand still
Teacher says - sit down
Teacher says - don't giggle
Teacher says - don't frown

Teacher says - read
Teacher says - add
Teacher says - good
Teacher says - bad

Teacher says - come here
Teacher says - go there
Teacher says - don't shout
Teacher says - don't stare

Teacher says - be quiet
Teacher says - who talked?
Teacher says - nothing
Pupil says - I'm shocked!

Nadine Fox (9)
Dalserf Primary School

HIP HOP

Hip! Hop! Wallty whop
Here comes Mum with my smelly socks
Here comes Dad with his big, black book
And here I come like a little sook

Hip! Hop! Knock! Knock!
Here comes Gran with her little box
Here comes Papa with is big, brown beard
And here I come, being a bit weird!

Hip! Hop! Wix and wax
Here comes the woodcutter with his little axe
Here comes big brother looking for a fight
I think I'll disappear like a clever little mite!

Alastair Walker (10)
Dalserf Primary School

THE WITCH'S LUNCH

Listen to the witch's brew!
Crickle! Crackle!
Chip! Chop!
Munch! Munch!
Gobble! Grunch!
Add a snake, plip, plip, plop,
What on earth is she having for lunch?

Ross Turner (9)
Dalserf Primary School

MY FAMILY

Vampire bats can suck your blood
And even kill you
Did you know I am a vampire bat
And my family too?

Killer sharks can kill you
Did you know I am a killer shark
And my family too?

Cobras can eat you
Did you know I am a cobra
And my family too?

A devil can bother you
Did you know I am a little devil?
My family say it too!

Greg Barclay (10)
Dalserf Primary School

MY BAD DRAGON

I have a pet dragon,
A green dragon with pink dots,
That can eat children,
So if you call me a bad name,
He will eat you up
And you will feel his fiery fangs
And this is not a game!

Dawn McConnell (10)
Dalserf Primary School

THE FUTURE

Buildings shaped like ice cream cones and stars,
Soap stars wearing jeans and T-shirts to go to nightclubs,
Children going to work and adults going to school,
People walking around with wacky hairstyles,
Mobile phones used as house phones,
People have monkeys as pets
Little boys wearing suits instead of jeans and joggies,
Little girls wearing sparkly dresses,
Pop stars wear horrible hats and have wacky hairstyles,
Aliens land on the planet and become our friends,
We use spaceships and flying saucers to get to school and work,
The 50s clothes are back in fashion,
Pets talk to their owners
We fly to Mars in spaceships,
No one does housework, so houses are messy,
We eat chocolate and ice cream for dinner,
Mums and dads let you ride their spaceship when you are seven,
In the future you can do anything.

Jennifer Neil (10)
David Livingstone Memorial Primary School

THE FUTURE

Spaceships flying through the sky
Buildings look extremely weird
Kids are flying about on their hover boards
Cars are talking to each other
Trees are walking along the street
Aliens are playing with their friends
People are walking on their ceilings
Water is shape-shifting by itself

Animals with more than two heads
People are walking through walls
Children are turning invisible
Pictures are coming to life
Mermaids are swimming in the sea
Houses are weird and funky
In the future anything is possible
That's my type of future.

Andrew Cox (10)
David Livingstone Memorial Primary School

A DARKENED LIGHT

Sitting on a bench, admiring the view
Watching the trees, rivers and clouds too
Splash, splash, the sound of the river
A distant echo of the birds' song
But all of a sudden, darkness fills the air
Clouds become evil to the world
Rain from above, getting wet
You hear the water moan like a painful cry
No more echo from the birds
Just the machine dumping in the river from above
I only hear the lonely cry of a solitary bird
Wiping her eye
Pollution fills the air
Like a dark, dark cloud full of despair
Sitting there with so many cares
I wipe my eye
As I listen to
The forlorn cry of mankind dying.

Euan Ronaldson (11)
David Livingstone Memorial Primary School

BEST FRIENDS

Best friends are fun
Best friends are nice
When I'm in trouble, I ask them for advice

Best friends make you feel good
Best friends make you look cool
I meet my friends every day at school

Best friends are great
When I'm late they wait for me at the school gate
I wouldn't live without them
If they weren't alive, my world would be dull

They are so good, I feel as if they are my family
They make me feel at home
I don't know what I'd do without them
They are my whole world

A medal, rosette, trophy and a bunch of flowers
Would never pay them back
For all the good things they have done for me

Maybe I'll just give them all my love
And ask them round for tea.

Kirsten Darling (9)
David Livingstone Memorial Primary School

THE POLLUTION

I walk alongside the clear blue lake,
As I walk I see little ducks quacking after their mother,
When I return I see black water like a bubbling swamp.
The beautiful scenery is turning into a nightmare.
What is happening?

The air smells like pollution.
The darkness begins to grow more and more.
I look and see a factory pumping chemicals into the lake,
The ducks are no longer here,
They have all died of the disastrous chemicals.

Lisa Rodmell (11)
David Livingstone Memorial Primary School

THERE'S SOMETHING UNDER MY BED

There's something under my bed
And it's scaring me
Who or what could it be?
There's a scuffing noise on the floorboards
All has gone silent but not for long
A soft, tiny scratching starts again
A small shadow flits in and out from under my bed
I'm getting very impatient, I want to find out what it is
But I'm scared to look under my bed
I'm sitting on my bed, biting my nails
Until there's barely a nail left
Still on my bed, silent and still
Thinking I'll need to find out!
I can't be a coward for the rest of my life
I creep to the edge of my bed, lean over and look under
My heart is beating like a drum
Should I shout for my mum?
To my delight it was not a big, scary monster
No need for me to be afraid
Just my old, hairy, lazy white terrier
Scruffy!

Lauren Munro (9)
David Livingstone Memorial Primary School

SEA LIFE IN DANGER

Imagine you're on a boat,
Out at sea,
Drifting happily and contentedly,
Then you see a path of oil in the sea,
The happiness is gone,
You are puzzled.
It suddenly strikes you!
The sea life in this area,
What will happen now?
Remember they live here,
Their homes are here,
Their families are here,
What must it feel like?
Trapped, suffocated and panic-stricken
That this has happened.
This is caused by a barrel,
Falling off an oil rig and exploding,
Or a ship,
A ship that is leaking.
It is simple things like this,
You need to care about.

Ryan Whyte (11)
David Livingstone Memorial Primary School

AT THE BEACH

I smell the salty seawater while I play with my beach ball
I taste the delicious vanilla ice cream as it touches my lips
I touch the soft sand as I build my huge sandcastle
I see everybody having a nice day at this great beach
I hear the screaming of all the playful children.

Nicola Rennie (9)
David Livingstone Memorial Primary School

COLOURS

Blue is the colour of the sky
and the colour of the Rangers top
and the colour of the carpet in my room

Green is the colour of the grass
and the colour of my record of achievement

Red is the colour of the roses
and the colour of my jotter

Yellow is the colour of the scorching sun
and the colour of the sand on the beach

Grey is the colour of a great shark
and the colour of the stones.

Stuart Thom (10)
David Livingstone Memorial Primary School

IN THE HAUNTED HOUSE

Up the street, round the corner, there is a house at the top of the hill,
No one lives there, everything is black, there is a mystery in there,
Out of sight,
Up the path of mud and stones, up the broken stairway to find a ghost,
You enter the world of darkness,
You're all alone in the haunted house, up the stairs the mystery holds,
Out of nowhere something throws you out,
You look in the window, there is someone holding a picture of you,
You get back into the house, up the stairs to a room,
You go through the door, the window is open,
Shadows close the door,
You're all alone in the haunted house, in nowhere,
Out of sight.

Amanda Burns (10)
David Livingstone Memorial Primary School

COLOURS

Purple is the colour of my bedroom carpet,
of flowers and heather.

Blue is the colour of my school sweatshirt,
of the sky and sea and my hands when they are cold.

Yellow is the colour of the big bright sun,
of daffodils in the wind and of my pyjamas.

Red is the colour of the rim of my glasses,
of pillar-boxes and Rudolf's nose.

Green is the colour of the long grass,
of the numbers on my clock and peas on my plate.

Orange is the colour of carrots,
of my favourite fruit and of the street lights.

Black is the colour of coal,
of the night sky and of my dog, Zak.

White is the colour of my mum's wedding dress,
of paper and of snow.

Lindsay Jane Murdoch (10)
David Livingstone Memorial Primary School

MY SCOOTER

My scooter has blue wheels
And blue handles,
I play on it every day,
I fall off my scooter
When I go fast,
I really like my scooter.

Kirsty Robertson (10)
David Livingstone Memorial Primary School

FAIRYTALE CREATURES

Once upon a time there were fairytale creatures
Some of them had very strange features
They lived at the very edge of the wood
And some of them were quite uncouth
Snow White and Cinderella are the radiant ones
And the lady who had lots of sons
If you went today to see Monsters Inc
You would come out of the cinema and think
Was that a good film by Walt Disney's son?
Well I thought it was really fun
I don't think Walt Disney's fairytale creatures are that bad
But if they were destroyed, I would be so sad!

Carly McPhee (10)
David Livingstone Memorial Primary School

THE FUTURE

Aliens with three heads going about,
Tidying up after you.
Houses like massive domes
And televisions built right into the walls.
People with six legs and four heads.
You don't need to pay for your things
In the shop, because it is free.
There are no cars on the road,
But they are small spaceships flying about.
There are no glasses to drink out of,
You just pour juice out and it goes into a figure of a glass.
The sea has no water because it has jelly surrounding it,
So you could just walk over it to get to the other side.

Ashleigh Larkin (10)
David Livingstone Memorial Primary School

THE MONSTER UNDER MY BED

The monster under my bed is hairy and tall
Compared to him I am so small
When this monster wants something to eat
He tries to nibble at my feet
At night I hear him growling and sniff
My brother says that he is a myth
No person can hear him, only me
Come to my bedroom at night and see
My mother will not believe me, neither will my dad
If they slept in my room, they would see the frights I had
Wait till they see his ugly face and hear his crackling laugh
They will not say I made him up like a graph
This monster is as evil as can be
I will look out for you, if you look out for me.

Nicola McPadden (9)
David Livingstone Memorial Primary School

WAR POEM

Look at those terrorists in Afghanistan
The lives they took in America
Why can't they just get on?
Then the world would be at trust
Those poor people sit at home
Feeling sad and all alone
When the planes crashed with a big bang
Their family's phone never rang
The towers melted away
While smoke belted out.

Suzanne Traynor (10)
David Livingstone Memorial Primary School

I LOVE . . .

I love when the hot summer sun beats down on me,
I love when I can play on the beach on a beautiful day,
I love to go out and play on my bike,
Oh how I love to play.

I would love to get whisked away on a flying carpet to an
imaginary land,
I would love to explore a wild rainforest
And see weird and wonderful animals,
Oh how I would enjoy it.

I love to dance to my music,
I love to go to my dance class,
Oh how I love to dance.

I would love to be a cloud and drift away peacefully,
I would love to be a panda because I think they are so cute,
I would, I would, I would.

Lauren McKenzie (9)
David Livingstone Memorial Primary School

THE GOLDEN SUN

The sun is shining in the sky
Its bright, bright light will soon die
At night I hear the silent sigh
Which also takes on the sun's slight cry
The night has come, I say goodbye
And the sun whispers like a frozen leaf
Sorry, but now I have to fly.

Cody Codona (10)
David Livingstone Memorial Primary School

MY RESTLESS NIGHT

When I went to sleep one night
I started to get a fright!
To make it worse, the sky was gloom
And inside my room was filled with doom
Then it came from under my bed
And I thought, What's all this stuff
Going through my head?
Then I started to toss and turn
And my head started to burn
For I started hearing someone rolling over to grab me!
What could it be?
I decided to make up my mind
That whoever this was, I would find!
And this time I got a fright
So I looked under and it was my dog
Having a restless night!

Erin Dean (9)
David Livingstone Memorial Primary School

MY PLAYSTATION

PlayStation, PlayStation
PlayStation, PlayStation, what would I do without you?
PlayStation, PlayStation, I think you're brilliant
PlayStation, PlayStation, you're the best
PlayStation, PlayStation, I love these games that you play
PlayStation, PlayStation, you make me happy when I'm sad
Because you're my PlayStation.

Liam McMillan (10)
David Livingstone Memorial Primary School

COCO THE CLOWN

As he comes in with big red shoes with laces tied in an enormous knot,
He trips over the mat with his big size tens, which don't even fit,
He has big, baggy trousers with blue polka dots all over them,
His blue and green top has a hole at one side of it,
He has a bucket full of water, he is heading for me,
He is going to throw it, can it be?
Wait a minute, he is going to throw it at me,
I think it is only confetti, phew!
Oh! His trousers have fallen down,
He has spotty orange pants,
He has a bright red flower in the pocket of his shirt,
I think I know this one, he told me to smell it,
But I ducked and he squirted a little two-year-old,
What a fun day at the circus.

Aimee Irvine (9)
David Livingstone Memorial Primary School

THE PIGEON LOFT

My dad has a pigeon loft,
He keeps his birds in there,
When he lets them out to fly,
They go straight up in the sky.
He sends them off to races
And waits for them to fly back home.
Wishing they come back in time
And win one of the top three places.

Steven Reid (10)
David Livingstone Memorial Primary School

MARCH

March is spring just starting, it's winning against winter,
Hot sun, can't wait.
March is my birthday and my dad's birthday too,
What a great month.
March is when the weather gets good
And my dad plays football with me.
March is when the lovely flowers grow in my garden,
My mum helps me plant them.
In March there is a clear blue sky,
As clear as the sea.
In March the snow is melting away.
In March there is a bit of wind,
So get those kites out.

Erin Kelly (10)
David Livingstone Memorial Primary School

WINTER WINDS

Making you get colder and colder
Making scary noises
The wind outside blowing the tree
Making the tree all different shapes
Making scary noises
Making you get colder and colder
Every second of the day.

Kayleigh Hughes (10)
David Livingstone Memorial Primary School

GUY FAWKES NIGHT

G uy Fawkes Night is fun
U nder the night's sun
Y ummy potatoes in the bonfire

F ireworks go off
A wait for the bang
W atch out, it's coming back down
K rackle goes the bonfire
E verybody claps
S ee the wood burn

N ever go too near
I t can burn
G o inside and eat your potato and
H ave a nice time until
T he next 5th of November comes.

Sarah Gormley (9)
David Livingstone Memorial Primary School

MY FRIENDS

All my friends are kind,
they help me when they can.
I know in my own mind,
that help is close at hand.

My very best friend is Thomas,
who likes to play with me.
We like to run around all day,
until it's time for tea.

Robert Gracie (9)
David Livingstone Memorial Primary School

WINTER COTTAGE

A redbreast robin tweeting on the snow-covered walls,
Frozen plants coming through the frosty snow,
Greyish snow coming from the snowy chimney,
Tiny snow mountains in the garden,
Huge patterned footprints in the garden,
White snow hanging from the bare trees,
Layers of snow sitting on the roof,
Wind howling as it goes past.

Martin Grove (11)
Glassford Primary School

WHITE WINTER

Crunch, crunch, crunch goes the snow as people walk past,
Trails of footprints in the snow,
Little robins twittering,
Beautiful snowmen that children enjoy building,
Trees lose their leaves and are covered with snow,
Children having snowball fights.

Stephanie Donaldson (10)
Glassford Primary School

STORMY SEA

Clouds gathering overhead,
Men staying inside,
Saying, 'I'll go tomorrow instead.'
It's roaring with thunder outside,

Waves high enough to go overhead.
Dangerous enough to drop a man dead,
Storming over rocks,
Splash, halfway up a cliff.

Ross Clacher (11)
Glassford Primary School

NIGHT-TIME FEARS

A lightning flash, a thunder clap,
The cool wind howls,
The night is black.
Creepy shadows appear from everywhere,
Mouldy hands jump out from under the bed,
To pull you down.
The bare floorboards creak as someone comes up the wooden stairs,
Someone or something taps the window,
As a bloodcurdling screech is heard,
Silent owl sweeping past.

Lorna Johnston (10)
Glassford Primary School

NIGHT-TIME FEARS

Strange noises petrify me as I lie in my bed,
My wild imagination makes me think that demons are going to kill me.
The house is filled with an eerie silence as I dream that my parents
                                         have been murdered.
Shadows of people look like ghosts getting into my dreams.
I don't want to fall asleep in case I have a ghostly nightmare.

Scott Kemp (11)
Glassford Primary School

WHAT A WINTER WONDERLAND

Snow-covered rooftops with a faint wisp of smoke coming
from the chimney,
Little robins twitter, perched upon leafless trees,
White, crunchy, flaky snow buries your feet as you walk,
Flowers with invisible heads droop low with snow,
The touch of snow so soft and flaky makes my body tingle,
Glistening snow is everywhere, smooth as silk, undisturbed,
Soft sound of banging window shutters,
Little robin sitting all alone, like a statue,
Everything is so quiet and peaceful,
A reminder of a heart-warming story.

Stephanie Speedie (11)
Glassford Primary School

STORMY SEA

Whirling waves rushing through torrential rain,
Crashing against rough, jagged rocks,
The clattering wind is roaring like thunder,
Screeching and squealing like the brakes on a car,
Stringy, soggy seaweed tangled in slippery rocks,
Noisy breakers making seagulls screech and fly away,
Flooding the sand and washing away beautiful shells,
Slowly and silently flowing waves drift smoothly into the distance,
The wind is now still and quiet as a mouse.

Rebekah Tait (9)
Glassford Primary School

NIGHT FEARS

The cars go by my window at night
Like a strong gust of wind.
Is it a monster or isn't it?
Lights in the hall flickering on and off
Like a torch giving a signal.
The television downstairs is on
Or is it aliens talking?
There's a gap between my bed and the wall,
Am I going to fall down and get eaten?
Water dripping from the gutter
Like a nail tapping on the roof.
Monsters at the window trying to get in.
Mum comes in and wakes me up.
I'm glad morning is here.

Laura McNiven (9)
Glassford Primary School

NIGHT-TIME FEARS

Frightened, listening to nocturnal owls hooting in the garden,
Scary nightmares come into my head,
Black bats flying back to their gloomy caves,
The floor covered with crawling spiders,
Lightning flashes on and off through my window,
Dogs knocking things over in the street,
Wild wind sounds like a twister,
Hairy moths flutter in and out of the open window.

Allison Marshall (9)
Glassford Primary School

SNOW

Walls are covered in icicles
that look like sparkling spikes.
Snow is falling softly
onto the sleeping flowers.
A house hides in a deep, warm corner,
blanketed with snow.
A robin sings
from the freezing cold wall.
Ice is crackling and snapping,
while the snowflakes land gently on it.
I feel as though magic is all around me.

Gillian Crozier (9)
Glassford Primary School

NIGHT FEARS

Hungry wolves at the end of my bed
getting ready to pounce.
Little, grey mice running up the wall.
Big, green, slimy monsters under my bed,
about to pull me with them.
Big spiders crawling everywhere.
My brother breathing very loudly.
Something is in my wardrobe,
about to jump out and eat me.
Suddenly I wake up
and everything is all right again.

Alan Dawson (8)
Glassford Primary School

SNOW

Icicles hanging like daggers,
Falling one by one into the snow.
Cosy fires sparkling and flickering in warm hearths.
Children throwing freezing snowballs.
Footprints disappearing like magic into the deep snow.
Rooftops glisten like diamonds in a fairytale.
Plants go to sleep for the winter.
The falling snow is silent,
While the robin redbreast chirps happily.
Like a picture on a Christmas card.
I feel happy and excited
When snow starts to fall.

Louise Fleming (9)
Glassford Primary School

SNOW

Church bells are ringing.
Heavy snow is dropping from the sky.
Children are on their sledges,
having fun.
Icicles hang from houses,
like dungeon spikes.
The red robin stands
in the ice-cold snow.
The bare trees are covered in snow,
till the branches are about to snap.
People are shivering in the cold,
but it makes me feel happy and excited.

Nicholas Smith (8)
Glassford Primary School

NIGHT FEARS

Wolves scratching at the end of my bed.
I can hear them breathing.
Shadows moving at night.
I have nowhere to hide.
Monsters under my bed trying to grab me downwards.
Slimy hands trying to grip me.
The television flashing at night,
Making me scared to wake up.
Monsters might be outside my door,
Making me scared to go to the toilet.
The door opens and my mum comes in,
Now I feel fine.

Calum Johnston (8)
Glassford Primary School

SNOW

Icicles hanging from walls
like sharp knives.
Heavy snow falling from the sky
onto the bare trees.
Small birds flying to warmer countries,
while tiny animals start to hibernate.
Sleeping plants are covered
in white, fluffy snow.
The snow landing softly on your nose,
it melts and trickles down your face.
A snowy day is just like a fairy tale.

Jack Fleming (8)
Glassford Primary School

SNOW

The cold, glistening snow
drops from the gutters.
Icicles like daggers,
fall and pierce the snow.
The wind whistles
through the bare trees.
Plants are covered in a blanket of snow
while they sleep.
Children make igloos
while the church bells ring.
The robin redbreast stands
by the snow-covered cottage.
Snow hangs on the branches.
Winter makes me think of a fairytale.

Nikki Andrews (8)
Glassford Primary School

NIGHT FEARS

The grey mice rattling between the walls,
It sounds like someone tapping on them.
Cars going past, make me think of robbers coming to get me.
Monsters at the bottom of my bed ready to bite me.
The shadows on the wall look like ghosts.
The toys under my bed make me think they are turning into monsters.
My teddy bears look like little furry insects.
Then I wake up and morning has come again.

Caroline Marshall (8)
Glassford Primary School

DOLPHINS

D olphins are cute and very smart.
O ut and in the hula hoops, doing lots of tricks.
L ively and beautiful, always having fun.
P eople see dolphins, swishing in and out of the waves.
H ere in Scotland you can't find dolphins, but in my dreams I can.
I n the ocean I can see different creatures and different features.
N ow that it's time to go, 'Bye-bye,' I said.
S aying, 'Bye,' it swam away and I said to myself, 'I'll see it
   another day.'

Charlotte Walton (9)
High Blantyre Primary School

PIGS

There is a pig in my house
The problem is he wants to catch a mouse

He rolls around in mud
What am I going to do with a pig in my house?

When he comes out of the mud
He rolls around the house

What am I going to do with a pig in my house?

Emma Aitken (8)
High Blantyre Primary School

AT THE BEACH

I walk to the beach getting ready to play,
When I jump in the water, I am going to stay.
Kids in the water, playing with a ball,
Kids in the water, splashing along.

I walk to Mum and Dad,
To see if I can go on the boats.
A boat goes past and makes big waves,
When I go off, I go away.

Ian Robertson (9)
High Blantyre Primary School

SCOTLAND

S   ad history
C   urvy hills
O   pen roads
T   o drive through
L   and is so lumpy
A   nd so rocky
N   ever, ever does Scotland get boring
D   o all the things in Scotland and it'll take you forever.

Julie Boles (9)
High Blantyre Primary School

A POLAR BEAR

A polar bear is white and no other colours
A polar bear is a good hunter
A polar bear is a good swimmer, to catch fish
A polar bear is cuddly and fluffy
A polar bear is rough when it's attacked.

James Taylor (9)
High Blantyre Primary School

PIGLET

Oh how pretty
Piglet loves to gaze
At the pretty flowers

It helps to pass away
Some lovely hours
He picks them in bunches

Take a pretty rose for example
Put it to your nose
It's like a shower
Of sweeteners popping out

He likes to hum
Turn the tum for his mum
Or take a daffodil
For a bright flower
He looks at that
It's worth his time
To give to his mum
She also likes to hum
So it is now that
Piglet goes to bed
Shuts his eyes
And puts down his head.

Jody Flannigan (8)
High Blantyre Primary School

A FISH

It goes in a tank full of water
Or it lives in the sea
It has gills
And it is a wet pet

It can go under the water
And swims
When it is under the water
There are other fish.

Mark McQueeney (9)
High Blantyre Primary School

CHEETAH

The cheetah runs, the cheetah runs to catch its prey,
The cheetah plays with its cute, little cubs all day,
The cheetah hides in the tall grass waiting for something to go past

The cheetah runs, the cheetah runs to catch its prey,
The cheetah plays with its cute, little cubs all day,
The cheetah gets shot by hunters, now it's dead.

Graham Russell (9)
High Blantyre Primary School

FROGS

Once I had a frog
He sat on a log
He ate flies all day
Once he met a lady frog
They both sat on the log
Then she laid spawn
Now I am stuck with all these frogs.

Ryan McDonald (9)
High Blantyre Primary School

THE HIPPOPOTAMUS

The hippopotamus
Sat on a stone
Shows her flat teeth
And her tonsils
And more walking in the mud
Splashing the dirt

She goes to bed
And yawns and snores
And in the morning
You'll hear a noise
The hippopotamus
Has woken once more!

Karen Young (8)
High Blantyre Primary School

THE ALLIGATOR

Snap! Snap!
Can you guess what I am?
That's right, an alligator.
I will wait anxiously day and night
For someone to have a swim in the lake
If I see someone passing by
I keep low, when you come in,
I wait for a moment, then I strike,
I will be coming for you, so beware.

Ryan Kelly (9)
High Blantyre Primary School

THE FOX

There is a fox
Comes out at night
To hunt for food
Such as rats
Owls come out at night
To look for food
It is such a shock
When you see an owl
And a fox killing animals
They stay out until morning
Then they go home
The owl brings a fur ball up
But the fox just sleeps all day.

Lisa Ireland (8)
High Blantyre Primary School

THE BEASTIE

The beastie is a Scottish moose
He tucks in nicely in his hoose
Ye had like tae keep him as a pet
But if ye drap him, he'll get wet
He'll be able tae hear ye wi his big ears
A lump o' cheese is his fave meal
But if ye take him tae yer bed
Ye might squash him, he'll drap dead
So ye'd better keep him away fae yer head
Or he'll scratch ye and bite ye on yer head.

Andrew Henderson (9)
High Blantyre Primary School

HAMSTERS

Tiny creatures
Live in cages
Can have babies
Go upstairs
To get to bed
The bed looks like
A little house

Bits of wool
Chewed-up bits
Of toilet roll

I'm going to buy a wheel -
I like to stroke
I like to feel

Running round like mad
Or sleeping in a corner
Nesting in a hole.

Carly Taylor (9)
High Blantyre Primary School

SUNSHINE

S   hiny and bright, sunny and sparkly, big and wide.
U   p in the sky, glaring and gleaming through the cloudless sky.
N   othing dull, but dazzling sun glittering bright.
S   unny and clear, glistening and gleaming.
H   oping for this again, the sun is blinding and gaudy too.
I   love the sun, just shining, huge.
N   othing but a big sun - clear over the pond.
E   verything is gleamy and sparkly because of the sun.

Christopher Lyon (9)
High Blantyre Primary School

CATS

There's lots of cats
In my house
Why? Is the question

I keep them because
Lots of them are strays
But now hopefully
I will find homes
In a nice, warm place

I went to the papers
And asked
Could they put in an article
They did
So people had them
And took care of them.

Ashley Pryce (8)
High Blantyre Primary School

NEWSROUND

N   ewsround is cool!
E   very day at 5:25
W   ars and fires
S   tories every day
R   eally cool!
O   n CBBC
U   will like it
N   ew inventions
D   aily news.

Jordan Tennant (9)
High Blantyre Primary School

MY HIDDEN TREASURE

My hidden treasure is my rabbit,
He is cute and cuddly,
I wish I could give him a hug,
But I would have to let him go.
My rabbit is named after a take-away,
His name is Nibble,
And my Papa Smith
Always wants to eat him.
Nibble's ears are small
And his feet are white
And soft all over.
He hops and jumps all day.
The first time I saw him,
I was excited but Nibbles was not.
When he goes down the stair,
He jumps in the living room
And behind the couch,
Behind the fruit bowl,
My hidden treasure is Nibble.

Steven Smith (10)
Lanark Primary School

DOLPHINS

See the dolphins in the sea
They swim so gracefully
Diving, spinning and splashing around
Swimming on the waves

See them with their families
Doing spins in the sea
Singing their sweet song of the sea and spinning while singing
Diving in and out of the water like an amazing creature.

Victoria Wilson (10)
Lanark Primary School

THE TRAIN AND THE DESTINATION

I got the creepy cobwebby train
There was a skeleton driving the train
I'm going insane
But that wasn't all, there was a witch and a zombie too
Now I really need the loo
But lucky for me the train stopped
I zoomed off that train, not looking back
Up a brick staircase
Into a creepy, wooden house
There is even a dead mouse
I was scared
Frankenstein opened the door
No more
I fainted
He took me to a torn chair with springs hanging out
I woke up with a shout
Out of the house, without a doubt
Get out of my way, you stupid cat
I won't be back, I'm sure of that!

Aimee Howland (10)
Lanark Primary School

WHEN MY FRIENDS FALL OUT WITH ME

When my friends fall out with me
I feel very sad
They walk away from me
And call me names

And when I'm in the house
I don't want to go out
In case they are there
They get more people to
Gang up on me
My mum tells me to just
Go out and play
And just ignore them
But I can't, I'm too scared.

Lauren Cosgrove (10)
Lanark Primary School

FOOTBALL

Celtic Vs Rangers, kick-off,
It's passed to Petrov in edge of box,
Petrov shoots, he scores, Celtic 1 Rangers 0,
The whistle blows for half-time, kick-off, passed to Numan,
Numan chips it up to Flo. Flo scores, Rangers 1 Celtic 1,
10 minutes to go and Henrick Larsson gets a penalty,
Henrick Larsson hits it to the right of the keeper
And scores, Celtic 2 Rangers 1,
Whistle blows for full time.

Steven Flynn (10)
Lanark Primary School

HOLIDAYS

Portugal, Spain, France
Are popular destinations,
But Florida is the best.

On the plane is really boring,
All you can see is clouds,
Oh look, a film is on,
This might take my mind off things,
But sadly it has not.

Oh look, we're landing now,
Hooray, now we're here,
It won't be long until we get to our hotel,
Oh no, we're taking a bus.

The bus is really boring,
But look we're at our hotel,
Now we're going to a theme park,
Oh, I'm really excited.

Wow, we're on a roller coaster,
This is really great,
Up and down, round and round,
Oh no, it has ended.

Sadly it is time to go home,
It will be boring compared to this,
I have had such a fun time here,
I'll be really sad to go.

Cara McAlindin (10)
Lanark Primary School

SCHOOL DAY

Boys run, girls giggle
Pencils on paper, squiggle squiggle
Go out early, come in late
Smelly lunches on our plate
Out to play, *hip hip hooray!*
Dance and skip, leave the classroom in a tip!
Free once more, we wish forever more
Bell ring, hear it ding
In we go, to and fro
Boys behind, being slow
Work again
Just the same
Feels like being in a mummy's tomb
I can't wait till I go home.

Wionna Fox (10)
Lanark Primary School

DOLPHINS

Dolphins leaping
over the waves,
lovely sight.

Peeping out of the waves are dolphins,
how could anyone be happier than I am today?

I'll live in a villa in Florida,
I'll get a new job where I work with dolphins.

Amy Gallacher (10)
Lanark Primary School

NO ONE KNOWS HOW MUCH

No one knows how much I want to go to Australia
And be in an Aussie soap
I could be in Home and Away
People talk all funny, strange and awkward too
All my friends could come and see me on a sunny day
We could go surfing and shopping too
I want to go to Australia
Because that's the way I am!

Zoe Prentice (10)
Lanark Primary School

MUSIC

M   usic is my life
U   nusual but true
S   ong or radio
I   prefer song
C   ause you can choose what to put on.

Lee Robb (10)
Lanark Primary School

DOGS

Dogs are cute,
I've got three,
They are lovely and fluffy,
Some are big, some are small,
But I still love them all.

Fiona Scott (9)
Lanark Primary School

FOOTBALL

Football can be a dirty game,
When players foul,
They usually get sent off
And all the crowd howl.

The footballer hits the crossbar,
From a difficult angle,
His shot is so powerful,
It makes the crossbar dangle.

The footballer scores a goal,
From a long throw,
The striker heads it by the keeper
And misses it because he is slow.

Fraser Campbell (10)
Lanark Primary School

SPRING

What could be nicer than spring,
All the birds begin to sing.
If it was winter, the chicks would freeze,
Now the squirrels come out of their trees.
The birds start to make their nests,
I think spring is the best.
The pretty flowers begin to grow,
Beautiful daffodils in a row.
The eggs start to hatch,
As their mothers rest in the thatch.

Emma Robertson (10)
Lanark Primary School

MY SISTER, JADE

I love my sister,
She's fun and cool.
She hits me,
I hit her back.
I don't mean to,
She just makes me mad.
I love her to bits
And she loves me too.
When my friends are over,
She annoys them, that's true.
She makes my mum and dad crazy,
But they love her too.
She's cheeky sometimes,
Now that's all I can say about her
Because she's only two.

Linzi Foster (10)
Lanark Primary School

HIDDEN TREASURE

Hidden treasure is everywhere
Hidden treasure is in the darkness, waiting to be dug up
Hidden treasure can be valuable, dangerous and disgusting!
Hidden treasure can be lying at the bottom of the sea
Hidden treasure can be cursed, waiting to kill
I wish I could find hidden treasure
It would be wonderful and amazing
I would not give it to a museum
If I ever find hidden treasure
I will be rich.

Ronan Turner (10)
Lanark Primary School

IMAGINATIONS

Imagination is a wonderful thing!
You can go to the moon,
I think I'll go to outer space,
I hope I go soon!

You can be whatever you want,
I'd be a dolphin, dog or pony!

My imagination is as good as it gets!
I've been to the bottom of the sea
And seen a mermaid!
I've been to another galaxy,
It was great fun!
I met aliens,
All green and lumpy!

I love my imagination!

Katie McGaan (10)
Lanark Primary School

GOALS

He runs, he shoots,
It's a goal!
It's a free kick, he crosses it in, heads it,
It's a goal!
It's a penalty, he runs up, he boots it,
It's a goal!
He passes, it's a one-two, he flicks it up, volleys it,
It's a goal!

Ruaraidh Gardner (10)
Lanark Primary School

FOOTBALL

It's Rangers Vs Celtic at Ibrox,
We have kick-off,
Fernando Ricksen running up the wing,
He crosses it in to Ronald De Boer,
Rangers score!
Larsson running up the wing, passes it to Hartson,
Konterman with a bad tackle,
Petrov scores a free-kick.
It's 1-1 at half-time,
They come back on, it's kick-off.
Larsson skins Flo and Ricksen he curls it round Konterman,
It's a great save by Klos, Klos throws it out to Arvesladze
And what a great goal,
It's 2-1 at full time, what a great game.

Darryl Cavers (10)
Lanark Primary School

FOOTBALL

Football is the game to play
It's played everywhere, I know
There is a match being played
Where the player passes to another player
And he runs up and he shoots
Goal!
The crowd go wild and the match ends
1-0.

Michael Coyle (10)
Lanark Primary School

HOLIDAY

Paris, Greece, London, France
Sun is fun
Holidays are the greatest
Holidays are great fun
Seeing all the famous places
Seeing all the famous buildings
Eiffel Tower, Blackpool Tower, building power
Beaches are fun, swim in the sea
And best of all, it's totally free
Rent a bike or go for a hike
Go to a park until it gets dark
And then go home
It's boring at home.

Gavin Alston (10)
Lanark Primary School

I WISH I HAD A DOG

Dogs are cute,
I draw them all the time.
Curly, fluffy, oh so fine.

I like my friend's little puppy,
He jumps and plays, sits and stays,
My friend is very lucky.

I wish I had a dog,
Big, small, I wouldn't care,
I wish I had a dog.

Jennifer Lang (10)
Lanark Primary School

FOOTBALL

It's time for the Aberdeen Vs Rangers match
It's time for the match
Referee Mike Curry blows the whistle and here we go
Lorenzo Amouroso kicks it out for a corner
Robbie Winters is taking a corner
It's punched away by Stefan Klos
It's a corner for Rangers
Lorenzo Amouroso skins Derek White
It's a goal for Rangers!
It's a goal from Lorenzo Amouroso
It went in top right-hand corner
It's half-time, it's Aberdeen 0 Rangers 1
The teams come back out
Rangers kick-off again
It's a penalty for Aberdeen
Robbie Winters puts it on the spot
This is to draw 1 each, oh what a goal!
It's 1 all
That's 90 minutes gone
And that's the end of the game.

Stewart Bell (9)
Lanark Primary School

MONSTERS

Monsters are scary and can be hairy,
They can be under your bed or in your head.
There's Frankenstein, Dracula, Mike Myres and more
And lots of them can make a lot of fright.
At night they're out, but during the day,
They all go away.

Robert Phillips (9)
Long Calderwood Primary School

OUR COOL SCHOOL

O ur school is cool, that's what it is
U s boys and girls are cool as well
R un a mile to come and see it

C ome on, you know you want to
O n the ball every day
O n the ball every night
L ove art, French as well

S cience is better than the rest
C halk dust on the floor
H ead teacher is Mrs Crawford
O ut in the playground's really cool
O ur school dinners are yummy too
L ong Calderwood is our school
    That's why it's *our cool school!*

Lorna MacPherson (10)
Long Calderwood Primary School

9 'TIL 3

Nine o'clock, the school bell rings
Boys and girls chatting about different things
Up to the classroom, one by one
Today we'll have some lessons, then it's fun, fun, fun
Back for some more lessons, then it's lunch
I've got chicken fingers, they're yum, yum, yum
3 o'clock and it's time to go home
Yippee, now I can play with my mobile phone
It's Saturday, *no school*, but back on Monday
I have to do my work now, bye.

Lisa McGraw (10)
Long Calderwood Primary School

MY GARDEN

My little garden is special to me
With its flower bed and its pear tree
Next there's the part for flowers and herbs
All of them taste absolutely superb
I'm really fond of my little pond
But how I wish my prize sunflower would grow
Will it? Won't it? Who knows?
I'm entering a contest for colourful flowers
Hopefully first prize will be ours
That's why my garden is special to me.

Catriona Murray (10)
Long Calderwood Primary School

MY PUPPY

Five little puppies, jumping up and down
Along came a little girl and took number one
Four little puppies, running round a tree
Along came a little boy and took number two
Three little puppies, playing hide-and-seek
Along came a little girl and took number three
Two little puppies, chasing a ball
Along came a little boy and took number four
One little puppy, sitting all alone
Until I came along and took my puppy home.

Luke Pryce (10)
Long Calderwood Primary School

DINOSAURS

I wish dinosaurs were alive, I would have a pet Tyrannosaurus,
He would talk to me although I would not understand,
He would take me to school, I would call him Rex.

Or I might have a Pteranodon so I would not need to walk,
I might even go up to the moon and see if it tastes like cheese
And I would get lots of fish for my tea,
But I hope no dinosaur eats me!

I might even have a Utahraptor with his great speed,
So I would never be late for *anything!*

Callum MacDougall (9)
Long Calderwood Primary School

COOL SCHOOL!

C   ool is our school!
O   ur school is cool!
O   ur school rules, it beats the rest!
L   et's have fun, our school is the best!

S   cience and art rules!
C   ool school!
H   ours of fun for everyone!
O   ur teacher is so fun!
O   ur school rules!
L   ong Calderwood is our school!

Sacha Louise Brammer (10)
Long Calderwood Primary School

MY GIRLFRIEND

My girlfriend is nice,
She has a few pet mice.
She is cool as ice,
She likes chicken fried rice.
She likes cola and ice,
But she hates Basmati rice
And she is scared of woodlice.
She is the nicest in the world
And I'm willing to pay the price.
I lost my driving licence,
She's that nice,
My girlfriend.

George Lawton (10)
Long Calderwood Primary School

THE TEDDY BEARS' PICNIC

In the deepest part of the woods
You will find the teddy bears
Getting ready for their picnic
There's teddy bears here
And teddy bears there
The teddy bears are all dressed, not bare

I went down to the woods, woods, woods
And I fell over a plank of wood, wood, wood
The teddy bears are having their picnic

I saw the teddy bears, the teddy bears
Are having their picnic.

Danielle Mitchell (9)
Long Calderwood Primary School

MY BEST FRIEND

M y best friend, she's lots of fun
Y ippee, together we run and run

B est she is, she is so great
E very day we play until late
S aturday night, I stay with her
T uesday night I play with her

F riends we are all the time
R unning and running, playing fine
I n and out we know each other
E very day we love to play
N ow this poem is nearly done
D ay is ending, it's not quite done
    But thanks, it's been lots of fun.

Stephanie Alexander (10)
Long Calderwood Primary School

HALLOWE'EN

'Oh, witches and wizard,
Where have you been?'
'We've been round the corner for old Hallowe'en.'
'A Hallowe'en party, what did you eat?'
'Burnt fingers, chicken legs and old frogs' feet.'
'After the food, what games did you play?'
'Witchcraft, paper plates and scaring them away!'

April Rankin (9)
Long Calderwood Primary School

TEACHERS

School is one thing,
But the teachers, 'Oh no.'
All they do is moan and groan,
But my teacher
Is not like that,
She is actually quite smart.
She is the best,
She is better
Than the rest.
She is gentle,
She is kind,
Being taught by her,
Well, I don't mind.
She makes us laugh,
She is so funny,
I hope they pay her
Lots of money.

Paula Copeland (10)
Long Calderwood Primary School

RAINY DAYS

I woke up this morning to the rain
It was driving me insane
On the way to school, it was plain
And then my tooth was in pain

My bike chain was rusty because of the rain
So I could not go and see my friend, Jane
So I stayed in the house, out of the rain.

Jamie Collins (9)
Long Calderwood Primary School

TEDDY DARES

I have a lot of teddy bears
And I make them do lots of dares
There's Daredevil Dan who jumped off a cliff
He's one hundred and one, old and stiff!
My French teddy, Flower
She jumped blindfolded off the Eiffel Tower!
Baby, Jus-Cus
Joined the circus
And was on again and again
People are always saying that baby's insane!
There's millions more teddies
But Mum's calling, 'Beddies'
Goodnight, 'Mum, tuck in my teddies!'

Sheryl McFarlane (9)
Long Calderwood Primary School

I'VE GOT CHORES TO DO

I've got chores to do
The dishes in the sink
I've got to make them shine and shimmer
But I'm going to make it look like slimy, old dinner

It's not fair, I've got chores
And no one else has!

Now I've to wash the floor, until it gleams
But I'm going to wash it with glue
So that feet stick to the floor
Now make me do more chores!

Nicole Hamilton (9)
Long Calderwood Primary School

UP THE HILL

Go up to the hill, sit down and stay,
Watch the busy world, see the horses play.
The sun is rising, it's smiling, isn't that surprising?
You feel for your most beloved locket,
In your jacket pocket.
The sun makes you think of your family,
The sun rose so calmly.
Look at the lovely flowers if you please,
Now you are at ease.
The roses have such spectacular poses,
Go up to the hill, sit down and stay,
Watch the busy world and the horses at play.

Caitlin Grace (10)
Long Calderwood Primary School

OUR SCHOOL

O   ur school is crazy.
U   p and up in maths we go.
R   eading is spectacular as well.

S   cience is cool too, so
C   ome to our school.
H   ome is boring compared to our school.
O   ur football team is just the best,
O   ur teachers are simple, not the best.
L   C is also the best, so come along to check out our school.

Chris MacDonald (10)
Long Calderwood Primary School

ANIMALS

Rabbits in their burrows
Birds in their nest
Camels riding slowly
Lambs being born
Elephants with floppy ears
Dolphins doing tricks
Snakes slithering about.

Rebecca Young (8)
Long Calderwood Primary School

HALLOWE'EN

Witches flying
Hallowe'en crying
Pumpkins smiling
Candles shining
Witches and wizards to be seen
On this great Hallowe'en!

Gemma Stewart (9)
Long Calderwood Primary School

I'M NOT SCARED OF ANYTHING EXCEPT . . .

I'm not scared of ghosts or ghouls
I'm not scared of rats or bulls
I'm not scared of anything except . . .
My evil looking teacher!

Mark McQueenie (10)
Murray Primary School

WWII

W e went into a WWII class
O ur scary teacher hit a task
R eally scary, Mrs Nicol, we
L ined up at the wall, we
D id spelling in class

W ork hard to be done
A ll the P6s were laughing
R ude kids were in trouble

S chool work was hard in class
C lass was very bad in the war
H alf the class were upset
O ur scary teacher, Mrs Nicol hated us
O ur work was hard
L ooking at the scary teacher

D id we get hit? No
A ll the kids were quiet
Y ou did not like it
S chool is bad in World War II.

Nicola Gillan (10)
Murray Primary School

AUTUMN DAYS

Lots of colourful leaves fall from the trees like floating feathers
Bundles of leaves are under the trees
Where children play and have great fun
While squirrels go through the woods
Looking for food
Most children stay inside
As the trees are bare and winter is near.

Nicole Gibson (10)
Murray Primary School

WINTER WONDERLAND

Children playing in the snow
Most of them having snowball fights
Inside the house, they're all warming up
Watching the colourful Christmas lights
Outside it's snowing and the winds are blowing
The ghost of St Nick is coming down our chimney
A flesh-eating monster who likes nothing better than to
Come down your chimney and eat you on a piece of bread and butter
He is only scared of one ghost to whom he does not boast
On Christmas Eve I stay in my room
Shuddering to think what would happen
Last time he came in my room
I chased him away with a broom
But sometimes he's not that much bother
Because he tries to eat my little . . .
Brother!

Marc Thomson (10)
Murray Primary School

MY FRIEND

My friend is alright, I guess,
Not! She's more like awful, because she leaves a mess,
Everywhere, she goes with me,
I throw things at her, hee, hee,
My friend is cool and kind,
She's usually stupid because she doesn't use her mind,
Her name is Jennifer, my best friend,
That's the end of my poem, the end!

Claire Hastings (11)
Murray Primary School

THE LITTLE MONSTER

There is a little monster,
Who comes to our class,
He's quite small to me,
But others say 'He's tall!'
He has blue fur
And green eyes,
He eats a lot of pies
And acts the fool.
He's my friend,
Who I call a tool,
He doesn't mind,
He is very kind,
That's my friend, the little monster.

Graeme Smith (11)
Murray Primary School

FLYING HIGH

F   lying in my little plane
L   eaving tropics and the rain
Y   ellow and orange birds crow
I   n the gales and winds that blow
N   orth, south, east and west
G   liding, soaring above the rest

H   igh above the little town
I   n my cockpit snug and sound
G   eronimo I shout as I dive down
H   ow I hope I don't hit the ground.

Libby Hoban (11)
Murray Primary School

AUNTIE MABEL'S WEDDING

I was a flower girl at Auntie's wedding,
That sissy veil, I couldn't see where I was heading,
We waited for an hour in front of the priest,
He was far too hairy and looked like a beast.
Then came the rings, my favourite bit,
Then from behind, the candles were lit,
All was forgotten at the party that night,
My granny's lips were not in sight!
When Auntie came from behind the door,
I thought she might fall through that floor.
Cutting the cake, that was the end of the party,
But he slipped and fell on my old uncle Marty,
Right into the cake, crushing a cat,
Then the cake went *splat!*
And that was the end of Auntie's wedding.

Rachel Steel (11)
Murray Primary School

WEIRD, BUT SMELLY

Fee fi fo pinkie
I smell something stinky
Is it Colin? Is it Mark?
One of them has done a f**t
Oh my goodness gracious me
What a whiff, eh-eh-ghee!
Get your gas masks
Get your gas masks
Before you get contaminated!

Colin Greeves (10)
Murray Primary School

MONSTERS

Lots and lots of monsters creeping in my room,
Big ones, small ones, boom, boom, boom.
Everyone is outside playing on the tree,
As all the monsters in the house are coming here for tea.

Slugs, slime,
Everything sweet,
Anything smelly, for that's all they eat.

As all the monsters have to leave,
When I turn around, it's then I see,
There's really nothing left for me,
After all the monsters came for tea!

Michael Kent (9)
Murray Primary School

OUR TEACHER

Our teacher's very tall
And I have a problem,
I cannot hear him,
He is very tall
And I am very small.
Tomorrow I hope he's not as tall,
Or I grow about six feet,
I dream of him chasing me round the school,
Then I wake up and have to go to school,
Oh no, I have to go through that again,
Help me!

Lorna Kyle (10)
Murray Primary School

A NIGHTMARE!

It is always nagging at me,
It never leaves me alone,
I hate it when it shouts at me,
As I sit as still as a stone.
It has four eyes and a long tail,
It screeches really long,
It always annoys me
And chants a silly song.
I see it every weekday,
It annoys me all the time,
It makes me really angry
And it's all covered in slime.
It creeps around the tables,
It only shuts up from time to time,
It never, ever gives up,
As it dribbles in slime.
It's crawling on the carpet now,
It's rolling on the floor,
It's gotten very hungry,
So it gobbled up the door,
It's my teacher!

David Woodhouse (11)
Murray Primary School

THE MONTHS

As green as the grass in every month, but winter.
Winter is white like in our month of January.
But January is sometimes warm like summer.
Summer is warm like spring.

Graeme Bogle (11)
Murray Primary School

IF ONLY I COULD FLY . . .

I wish I had my own pair of wings,
To fly up into space,
I'd reach up to the highest star,
This idea is ace!

I'd swoop right up past Neptune
And circle round the sun,
I'd get very dizzy,
But it would also be very fun!

Then I would fly to Mars
And I'd land in a crater,
I'd explore the whole planet
And set off for Earth a bit later!

Here I am, back down on Earth,
What an adventure it was,
I would go back into space again,
These wings are the cause!

Susan Gardiner (10)
Murray Primary School

AIDAN

I have a baby brother,
Who really is no bother,
He sleeps most of the time,
It can't be a crime,
He is so cute,
He can't be a brute,
I love my baby brother,
Who really is no bother.

Kayleigh Hill (11)
Murray Primary School

THE DOLPHIN

The sea is full of wonderful things,
Starfish, crabs and lots more things.
My favourite is the dolphin,
It swims delightfully in the sea.
It splashes and jumps, I wish it was me.
They're intelligent and beautiful,
There are many types - bottlenose and whale dolphin,
I can think of more.

Grey and blue, whatever the colour,
You can get them in the sea,
I wish I could see them every minute of the day.

Alyesha McEwan (10)
Murray Primary School

THERE'S A MONSTER IN MY CLOSET

There's a monster in my closet
And a vampire in the juicer
There's devils on the ceiling
And ghosts in the sink
And a beast in the shower
And the scariest one of all is the
Monster in my closet, but
I think he's quite nice, but
My wee sister thinks
He's really scary and the other monster is
Me!

Sean Massie (10)
Murray Primary School

EARLY IN THE MORNING

Early in the morning is my favourite time
When the grass is wet and full of dew
As you step out onto the path
You can smell the freshness of the air
You can actually taste and feel it
Walk though the gate and feel the sun's heat beating down
On the small, colourful village in the middle of the valley
Watch the flowers dance in the gentle breeze
Hear the waterfall dripping and splashing down on the lake
Hear the birds chirping from above
This is the sort of scenery I love!

Catriona Meechan (11)
Murray Primary School

THE WEATHER FORECAST

The weather forecast yesterday was rain
The weather forecast today is sunny
The weather forecast tomorrow will be snow
Or maybe it will be winds that blow

When it rains the grass goes soggy
When it's sunny the birds are singing
When it snows the land is white
And when the trees are blown by the wind
It's not a pretty sight.

Jennifer Crawford (11)
Murray Primary School

THE NEAR LAND

I could see the morning dew
The birds were chirping happily
In the magic land I never knew
I had only been there a short while
And had immediately fallen in love
With my surroundings
The beauty of the flowers made me
Force out a satisfied smile
The lush, green field smelt freshly of springtime
And the squirrels were playing pleasantly
The bark of the tree trunk
Felt very fine
In the distance I saw the sun set
Which turned the sky a shade of warm pink
I wouldn't move from my position
I couldn't, not yet
A fantasy land had come to life
In my very own back garden . . .

Eleanor Turner (11)
Murray Primary School

TICK-TOCK

Tick-tock
Goes the clock,
Tick-tock,
Even when you're sleeping.

Tick-tock,
Time passes away,
Tick-tock,
For it's not here to stay.

Stevan Harris (11)
Murray Primary School

THE ZOO

I went to the zoo
And saw a cuckoo,
The monkey stood on his head,
The hippos were funny
And so was the bunny,
The pig wouldn't come out of its bed.

Daddy got bitten
By a big kitten,
As he alone calls it,
It was indeed a lion,
Whom at Dad kept on starin',
So it nearly took his hand with it.

Mummy was silly,
As she saw a goat called Billy
And then she fed it some grass,
She got a bit hyper,
So Dad sat down beside her
And then we went to see the ass.

That concludes my trip to the zoo,
My favourite was the cuckoo,
It was very funny,
Besides Mum being hyper
And Dad sitting beside her,
My second favourite was the bunny.

Emma Wilkie (10)
Murray Primary School

SLITHERING SNAKES

Slithering snakes,
Slimy and sleek,
Slim and sneaky,
Smoothly moving,
Round your feet!
Do not cry,
Do not squeak,
Because it will crush you like wheat!

Sean Swindells-Dallas (11)
Murray Primary School

MY ADVENTURE

Mrs Miller thinks I am working,
But I am having an adventure,
Looking for some treasure.
I am now in a cave,
With a hairy, big bear,
I have to fight him to give him a scare.
I'm in the ocean with a dolphin,
He gave me a ride to his home,
I stay there for a while,
They show me the treasure
I am looking for,
Boring! Back in the class,
Listen to the teacher,
I might go back another day
For an adventure.

Kelly Jackson (11)
Newfield Primary School

THE MERMAID

Mrs Miller thinks I'm working,
She's looking right over at me,
But I'm not listening,
I'm dreaming that I'm under the sea,
The water's streaming through my hair.
Just then I feel a tug at my foot,
I feel a pearl chain tugging round my neck,
Then I see a chunk of long, golden hair.
I feel a soft hand holding onto mine,
I look around and notice it's a mermaid,
She asks me what I want to do,
I said I want to be with you,
I still remember that dream,
I wish I could go there again!

Gillian Lambie (11)
Newfield Primary School

MY DAYDREAM

Mrs Miller thinks I'm writing
But No
I'm in a deep dark cave
I'm on a quest to find hidden treasure
I look, look and look but I can't find the treasure
I see something shining
It was the sun's rays shining on something gold
When I wake up everybody shouts
'Wake up!' Then I'm back in the classroom
Not in my wonderful dream anymore
What a lovely treasure chest that was.

Shahla Mirbakhtiar (10)
Newfield Primary School

HIDDEN TREASURE

Mrs Miller thinks I'm working,
But I'm not, I'm daydreaming,
When I walk upon the pirate's ship
And look for hidden jewels,
I see something shiny,
That's a chest full of hidden gold.

Kimberley Walker (11)
Newfield Primary School

MY TASTY DAYDREAM

Oh the hamburger, what a brilliant taste,
My mouth waters once you come out of the oven.
I cover you in tomato sauce,
As I bite into you, I get tomato sauce on my mouth,
So warm and tasty in my mouth,
I will always enjoy a tasty burger.

Liam Thomson (10)
Newfield Primary School

SPICY CHICKEN PIZZA

Spicy chicken pizza, sitting there in a warm pizza box
Ready for me to open and eat it all up

Its golden chicken taste with sauce
And melted-on cheese, melting in my mouth
I can't wait to have a slice of the delicious, spicy chicken pizza.

Steven Forrest (11)
Newfield Primary School

I'M DREAMING OF THE SEA

Mrs Miller thinks I'm working,
But I'm actually asleep,
Thinking of the seabed,
Look what I see, red, red rubies,
I've found a golden chest,
Full of the best crystals and diamonds you could ever see,
But then I just realise I've found gold, gold and more gold,
As I get more excited I wake up,
Mrs Miller says, 'Are you working?'
'Yes,' I said.
My adventure was just a daydream.

Laura Thomson (11)
Newfield Primary School

ADVENTURE

A   rchaeology is a wonder
R   ough cliffs and lush green rainforests
C   old, snowy Arctic
H   ot or cold, does not matter
A   lovely meal inside my tummy
E   very day nearly starving
O   h, how long roads, go on forever
L   ong, winding roads
O   h, the sunshine
G   old and silver is every man's dream
Y   e wild world lies a mystery.

Catriona Harkness (10)
Newfield Primary School

MY SWEETIE DAYDREAM

Mrs Miller thinks I'm working,
But I'm caught up in a daydream,
I am stranded on an island,
I approach a ship down
A really big dip,
I've got the key,
I float right over
And there it is a
Treasure chest full of sweets,
I wake up, I have to run quick,
I feel so sick,
After all those sweets.

Adele Mitchell (11)
Newfield Primary School

A HOT DOG

One little treasured hot dog
    sitting on a table
Waiting for me to come in
    and have a *bite!*
Lovely and warm
    with tomato ketchup
The roll is so smooth
    I love it all
I can't wait to taste it
    so yummy and warm
The treasure is eaten now!

Graeme Lindsay (11)
Newfield Primary School

MY FAVOURITE DAYDREAM

I awake from my sleep,
But I don't know where to go.
So many events
And so much, I don't know.
I see a flying crab, with wings
And magical claws,
But I awake from my dream,
Chewing on drinking straws!

Graeme Copland (11)
Newfield Primary School

I WAS IN A DAYDREAM

I was in a daydream,
Dreaming of a chest full of coins,
The teacher thought I was doing my work,
Silver and gold coins,
The school bell rang, I woke up,
Everyone ran away,
What a day!

Laura Hinshelwood (11)
Newfield Primary School

THERE ONCE WAS A PANDA

There once was a panda, who went to visit his granda,
He took him to the park, aboard Noah's Ark,
Then a dog went *bark* and it began to get dark
Then he went home to have an ice cream cone.

Conor Meechan (8)
Our Lady Of Lourdes Primary School

IF I WAS A KID

If I was a kid I would stand and play,
As if I had all the time in the world, not just a day.

If I was a kid I would play with my dolls,
Dress them up, but not them all.

If I was a kid I would play ghosts and ghouls,
Even at school!

If I was a kid I would watch Barney,
Sing along, hard? Hardly.

If I was a kid I'd be nice to Mum,
Not say, 'You're dumb' or 'You've got a big bum.'

Laura Jackson (9)
Our Lady Of Lourdes Primary School

WINTER FEELINGS

Fat snowman, bright moon
Sharp icicle, thin logs

Bare trees, frozen cars
Jagged evergreen, cold snowflakes

Hot soup, sweet turkeys
Smelly candles, small pies

Raw air, hot chocolate
Strawberry ice cream, juicy chicken

Singing birds, freezing wind
Christmas bells, Christmas.

Daniel Bree (10)
Our Lady Of Lourdes Primary School

WINTER FEELINGS

Bare branches, glowing fires
Decorated snowmen, swirling snowflakes
Shining in the winter sun
Frozen cars, spooky trees
Sharp evergreens, hungry birds
Warming soup, scrumptious pudding
Steak pies, delicious turkey
Straight out the oven
Appetising gateau, hot chocolate
Tasty sweets, sweet honey
Laid out on the colourful table
Christmas carols, clanging bells
Singing robins, tuneful singers
In the silver glowing streets.

Christopher Martin (11)
Our Lady Of Lourdes Primary School

CRAZY COUNTING POEM

One skinny snake ate a fat cake,
Two wooden wagons ran over two big dragons,
Three little lizards ate fat wizards,
Four white sharks sat in all the parks,
Five black tables sat on a stable,
Six big beasts ate their feasts,
Seven dead fish lay on a china dish,
Eight little rockets crashed into my pocket
Nine fat kings sat on the swings
Ten fat dogs ate some frogs.

Andrew Behan (11)
Our Lady Of Lourdes Primary School

WINTER FEELINGS

Bare branches, singing birds,
Smooth snowdrops, icy lakes,
Shining with ice.

Cold robins, hard leaves,
Fluffy snow, sharp ice,
Melting in my hand.

Sweet soup, scrumptious turkey,
Delicious pudding, strawberry candles,
Flickering in the darkness.

Appetising apple, chocolate sweets,
Tasty gateau, raspberry cake,
Tasting very good.

Ringing bells, carol singers,
Wishing wind, angry cars,
Skidding in the slush.

Lynelle Brown (11)
Our Lady Of Lourdes Primary School

TIME

What is the time?
What is the date?
Is it early? Is it late?
Is that the time? My how it flies,
It is 10 o'clock so close your eyes.
Now it is the morning, so comb your hair,
Have your breakfast and put on your underwear.
Is it morning? Is it night? I just can't get the time right.

Stacey Gray (8)
Our Lady Of Lourdes Primary School

NATURE

As I see the butterfly fly over the sky
Then suddenly out the corner of my eye
I stand there, watch the spider die

I feel like I'm going to cry
But then I remember he's going up to God

I feel much better now
Because he's going to somewhere better

Now I stand there, watch an ant crawl over the grass
While I let a snail crawl over my nail

Even though I've just watched a cat kill a rat
And watched the insects do what they do
I stand there
And remember, that's just nature.

Stacey Davis (8)
Our Lady Of Lourdes Primary School

SPIDER TO A FLY

I'm a hairy black spider
I catch flies in my web
So don't get caught in it or you'll be dead
I've got 8 hairy legs to crawl fast up the wall
Be careful, look out, I'm scurrying down the wall
I might be hiding in the attic
Or hiding in the garden
And if I run into you, you'll beg my pardon
So here is a warning to you Mr Fly
The only safe place is up high in the sky.

Eilidh McCole (8)
Our Lady Of Lourdes Primary School

IT'S NOT FAIR

Leaving the fridge door open for everyone to see,
Unwashed dishes overflowing in the sink,
Spilt juice like a river on the floor
It's not fair, it wisnae me!

Loud music screaming in my room,
The light is on to run out,
Bed not made, my pillows everywhere,
It's not fair! It wisnae me!

Piles of toys on the floor,
TV is on too loud again,
Rabbit is ripping the suite,
It's not fair, it wisnae me!

Sticky soup on the floor,
Leaving the window open for everyone to see in,
Towels on the floor,
It's not fair, it wisnae me!

Matthew Allan (11)
Our Lady Of Lourdes Primary School

BEST FRIENDS

My friends and I, we love to play,
Upon a lovely day,
We love to dance and sing and shout,
We love to laugh and run about
And at the end of the lovely day,
We only have goodnight to say!

Lynsey Whyte (8)
Our Lady Of Lourdes Primary School

MY CAT

Black cats
Brown cats
White cats too
When my cat purrs
I think of you
Do you want a cat?
Well, you're not getting mine
My cat's black and furry too
I love my cat, do you like him too?
If you like him
Then
I like you.

Michael McCluskey (8)
St Cuthbert's Primary School, Hamilton

MY DOG, SHADOW

My dog, Shadow
Has black fur
Long legs too
Short tail
He loves playing
He hates sleeping
He eats Butchers dog food
He loves milk
And loves treats
I love my dog
Shadow.

Nathan Cairns (8)
St Cuthbert's Primary School, Hamilton

THE SNOWMAN

On Sunday it snowed.
On Monday the snowman said 'Hello.'
On Tuesday he played with me.
On Wednesday he said 'Goodbye.'
On Thursday he was gone.
On Friday I was sad.
On Saturday it snowed again.

Marianna Ames (8)
St Cuthbert's Primary School, Hamilton

THE FUNFAIR

I see good rides and big boats
I hear people scream and sweet music
I smell hot dogs and hamburgers
I touch soft toys and dogs
I taste sweet candyfloss and sweets
I feel excited.

Rebecca Crowley (7)
St Cuthbert's Primary School, Hamilton

PLANETS

I can see the planets all around me,
Look! Look!
An alien,
'Take a picture!'
I hear it cry.

I see space rocks on the ground,
The dust on Mars,
I feel tired from travelling.

Sean Titchmarsh (8)
St Cuthbert's Primary School, Hamilton

HAPPINESS IS ...

Happiness is when my cat bites my fingers
Happiness is being at home
Happiness is when I don't get homework
Happiness is when I get sweets
Happiness is when I see my friends
Happiness is when I go to the beach.

Sean McFall (8)
St Cuthbert's Primary School, Hamilton

AT THE CIRCUS

The talented acrobats glide across the room
The lion roars hungrily from his cage
I can smell the crunchy popcorn from the popcorn stand
I eat fluffy candyfloss
I can taste the hot dogs from the hot dog stand
I feel very happy.

Robyn Hannaway (8)
St Cuthbert's Primary School, Hamilton

FOOTPRINTS IN THE SNOW

Look at that!
Look at that!
Footprints!
Footprints in the snow,
I wonder why.
I wonder who.
Little children's footprints.
My! My!
They will be frozen.
Leading to the forest.
I hope they will be found soon.
I wonder why they went.

Amanda Cunning (8)
St Cuthbert's Primary School, Hamilton

ON A FARMYARD

Gentle cows being milked in the barn
Noisy chickens laying eggs
Baby calves mooing in the field
Shy horses neighing in their stable
Fried sausages sizzling in a pan
Mucky pigs playing in the mud
Crispy straw and hay
Curly, pointed pigs' tails
Fresh eggs being cooked
Fresh cow's milk in a huge jug
I feel happy but tired.

Roisin Gallacher (8)
St Cuthbert's Primary School, Hamilton

THE SEASIDE

Jellyfish under the water
Children playing on the sand
Children splashing in the water
Children screaming on the shore
Hot dogs at the hot dog stand
I smell tomato sauce
A jellyfish on the sand
Seaweed on the shore
A sandcastle
Smooth in
The salt water
A drink of juice
I feel happy and warm.

Gemma McGlynn (8)
St Cuthbert's Primary School, Hamilton

TIME

When I am doing nothing, time is slow,
But when I am enjoying things,
The time just seems to go
Flying by, like birds in the air,
When my mum is doing my hair,
Time just stands still
Like a very old chair,
But
When I'm swimming,
The time goes by like the wind.

Kerry O'Neill (8)
St Cuthbert's Primary School, Hamilton

THE CIRCUS

I went to the circus
To see the clowns
To eat the popcorn
To hear the horn
To see the acrobats
To taste the hot dogs
To laugh and laugh
To hear the barking of the dog
To see the juggler, juggle his balls
To hear the roar of a lion
To see the lion tamer, tame the lion
To hear the trumpeting of an elephant.

Matthew McCarroll (8)
St Cuthbert's Primary School, Hamilton

I WISH...

I wish I could jump very high
So I could look over the clouds
I wish I had gills
So I could swim underwater
I wish I could fly over the moon
I wish I was rice so I could be eaten
I wish I was a vampire
So I could bite
I wish I was a butterfly
So I can fly away.

Fraser Flannagan (8)
St Cuthbert's Primary School, Hamilton

ANIMAL HOMES

If you go down a hole
You may find a rabbit,
Spider,
A worm
Or a mole.
If you go in the water,
You would find
A tadpole,
You wouldn't find
A rabbit,
A spider,
A worm
Or a mole.
In a tree you'd find
A squirrel,
You wouldn't find a bumblebee.
In a pond
You'd find a duck,
You wouldn't find
A chicken,
Cluck.

Nicole McLean (8)
St Cuthbert's Primary School, Hamilton

MY CAT, O'MALLY

My cat, O'Mally
Has short legs
And orange fur
He likes to sleep all day.

Paddy Joe Gallacher (8)
St Cuthbert's Primary School, Hamilton

THE SEASIDE

Little children eating ice cream
Building sandcastles
Seagulls calling from the air
Waves crashing on rocks
Hot dogs burning on a hot dog stand
The smell of strong, salty seaweed
Coming from the sea
A slimy crab's shell
Cream on my arms
Rough sand on my little toes
Cold water, freezing children
Salty water in my mouth
I'm sleepy and happy.

Vhairi Kennedy (8)
St Cuthbert's Primary School, Hamilton

CASTLES

Shiny chainmail,
A jewelled crown,
Swords rattling hard,
People shouting for help,
Blood of dead soldiers,
Smoke from a fire,
Arrows,
Roast chicken served with fruit,
The weight of a sword,
The weight of all their weapons,
Now ruined and ancient.

Devran Babat (8)
St Cuthbert's Primary School, Hamilton

AUSTRALIA

Ayres Rock
Glowing in the sun
Not much life there
Fish splashing in the sea
Sand on my feet
The sea air going to my head
How little water there is.

Sean McQuade (8)
St Cuthbert's Primary School, Hamilton

IN THE GARDEN

In the garden trees and flowers grow,
Wonderful things come from the seeds I sow.
Daisies grow like little, white paint drops,
Willow trees hang like huge, grey mops.

There are birds in the trees singing sweetly,
There are flowers in the flower beds growing neatly.
Ivy and honeysuckle creep up the wall,
Towering sunflowers rise very tall.

Lilies, the colour of cream,
Clear blue water runs down the stream.
Blood-red roses under the light of the sun,
Watch the fluffy squirrels and rabbits run.

Apple trees and pear trees, trees of every kind,
Plants of every colour you can think of in your mind.
Sweet smelling lavender, tulips and heather,
The garden is beautiful in all sorts of weather.

Laura O'Neill (10)
St John The Baptist Primary School, Uddingston

THROUGH MY MAGIC DOOR

Through my magic door
There's a land of dragons
Strange and scaly ones
With enchanted stares
And deep, deep looks

Blood-red
They have fiery breath
I wish I was there

Some small ones
Some giant ones
Some middle-sized ones
There are scary ones
And some sweet ones
I wish I was there.

Paul Shaw (7)
St John The Baptist Primary School, Uddingston

THE NEW KID IN SCHOOL

There is a new kid in school,
His mum thinks he's a jewel.
She calls him her diamond in the rough,
Because he acts so tough.

He's always looking for a fight,
He thinks he's always right.
But he really is just a fool,
Who thinks he is so cool.

He gets into trouble every day,
He only comes to school to play.
We don't know what the teacher thinks of him,
Maybe she thinks he is so dim.

One day the teacher yelled,
'You are going to be expelled.'
He ran out with tears in his eyes,
Because he had been cut down to size.

Kevin Clements (10)
St John The Baptist Primary School, Uddingston

THROUGH MY ENCHANTED DOOR

Through my enchanted door
I can see a land of dragons
They are golden and very shiny
Some blue ones fly
Through the air

I wish I was there

Through my enchanted door
I can see some fiery red ones
With sharp teeth and claws
It is dark, I see pure white eggs
In a nest, glimmering golden dragons
Back at their nests

I wish I was there.

Steven Kelly (8)
St John The Baptist Primary School, Uddingston

THROUGH MY MAGIC DOOR

Through my magic door I can see
Fairyland
In fairyland
There are little colourful fairies
Shopping and playing everywhere you go
Fairy dogs and fairy cats
I wish I was a fairy

I can hear fluttering wings
As they hurry about their business
The little fairies sing and dance
Cheerfully leading the band
As soon as they saw me it all went quiet
Then looked at me happily and cried,
'Hello,'
I wish I was a fairy.

Corra Brown (8)
St John The Baptist Primary School, Uddingston

THROUGH MY MAGIC DOOR

Through my magic door I can see
Hundreds of eyes staring back at me
Dancing pixies
Singing sweet songs
Laughing elves
Playing happily
I wish it was me

Through my magic door I can see
Lots of teeny tiny people
Friendly fairies
Sprinkling shiny magic dust
All of them wear funny hats
And dance gleefully
I wish it was me.

Nicola Ward (8)
St John The Baptist Primary School, Uddingston

THROUGH MY MAGIC DOOR

Through my magic door I can see
A land of creatures from the world
Slimy pythons
Slithering and snapping
Scary lions
Running and pouncing
I wish I was there

Through my magic door I can see
Swooping owls
Chasing field mice
Tiny humming birds
Singing in their trees
Wrinkly lizards
Scampering along the ground
I wish I was there.

Ryan McGill (8)
St John The Baptist Primary School, Uddingston

A VIEW FROM MY WINDOW

The light was flashing on and off.
The trees were swaying very soft,
They were very quiet, not making a sound.
The leaves were dancing across the ground.

The burn was flowing. It was crystal clear,
It was moving quickly like a running deer.
I looked at the road, it was dull and black,
It was shining too like a big bin sack.

The grass was spiky, gloomy and wet,
I saw the green bushes so neatly set.
The path was dirty, covered in brown leaves,
As they skipped along with the breeze.

When I saw this, it was so much fun,
But then my mum called up, so I needed to run.

Georgia Sami (10)
St John The Baptist Primary School, Uddingston

LOOKING THROUGH THE DOOR

Looking through the door I can see
Twinkle, twinkle little stars
Glistening off the passing cars
Dashing here and dashing there
Hopefully going to get them there.

Zara Nicholson (8)
St John The Baptist Primary School, Uddingston

THROUGH MY DOOR OF FANTASY

Through my door of fantasy I can see
Hansel and Gretal
Wandering through the forest all alone and tired
Alice in Wonderland
Trying to find her way home from the magnificent maze
Through my door of fantasy

Through my door of fantasy I can see
Cinderella
In her dazzling ball gown rushing back from the ball
The Three Bears
Walking through the forest, waiting for their breakfast to cool
Through my door of fantasy.

Laura Kilgour (8)
St John The Baptist Primary School, Uddingston

ON CHRISTMAS NIGHT

On the night before Christmas everywhere,
All the children begin to prepare,
For Santa arriving with presents galore,
While they sleep and gently snore.

They hang up their stocking and prepare a feast,
For Santa Claus and Rudolph, his beast!

Upstairs they go and climb into bed
And sleep when their pillow touches their head!
All mummies and daddies put out the light,
Say, 'Goodnight little on, sleep tight!'

Ashleigh Corbett (10)
St John The Baptist Primary School, Uddingston

THROUGH MY MAGIC DOOR

Through my magic door I can see
Bubbling cauldrons with witches around them making a brew
The cackling laughter and hooked noses
So horrible when they look at you
Cobwebs everywhere with spiders on them
Crawling on your head and up your face
While gruesome witches with sagging skin
Look at you and grin

Their teeth are black and dirty
Their fingers are long but skinny
Their black, piercing eyes stare at me
From under their long, black fingers
They fly on their whizzing broomsticks
In the dark night sky.

Rachel Burns (8)
St John The Baptist Primary School, Uddingston

ANGEL

Angel is a friendly beast,
Chocolate is what she calls a feast.
She wears two pigtails either side of her head,
She wears a long dress that is ruby red.
She has three eyes, they are all blue,
This means she can see you.

She has wings like a butterfly,
If you call her names, she will cry.
Angel's wings are pink and blue,
I am her friend and so are you.

Sara Begley (10)
St John The Baptist Primary School, Uddingston

THROUGH MY MAGIC DOOR

Through my magic door I can see
Dragons
Breathing out boiling hot fire
Stomping down houses
Eating people up
Flying in the sky
Eating all the birds
I am glad that dragon can't see me

Through my magic door I can hear
Dragons
Squealing for some food
With their bellies rumbling and gurgling
And their jaws bashing together
I am glad that dragon can't see me.

Kevin Izat (8)
St John The Baptist Primary School, Uddingston

THROUGH MY MAGIC DOOR

Through my magic door I can see
A monster peeking in at me
Hairy and red with fireballs in his head
A monster staring in at me
His eyes are as big as a frog's shell
His body as big as a bear
Should I run away and slam the door
Or hide and spy on him?
A monster glaring in at me.

Ruairidh Gallagher (8)
St John The Baptist Primary School, Uddingston

THROUGH MY MYSTIC DOOR

Through my mystic door I can see
Creatures from the plains
Tall lionesses
Creeping, then sleeping
Thin, slim prairie dogs
Digging underground
I wish I was there

Through my mystic door I can see
Sneaking hunters
Seeking innocent lions
Black people
Practising hunting dances
Silly farmers
Growing crops in the wrong places
I wish I was there.

Ruth Brandon (8)
St John The Baptist Primary School, Uddingston

THE SEA

Crashing like the waves against the parting rocks,
Wild as the wind, that whips my cheeks and mocks.
Roaring like the rain stinging in my ear,
Squawking like the lost birds, that no one can hear.
Rushing like the current, breaking things apart,
Flashing like the lightning, breaking in the storm's heart.
Angry as the thunder crashing through the sky,
Raging like the waters as they flow by.

Aileen Larkin (10)
St John The Baptist Primary School, Uddingston

THE HIPPO BALL

What's that I see? Oh what can it be?
Moving past the nearest tree,
It's underwater, so I can't see,
What it is that's staring at me?
A rock that's moving, but how can it be?
I begin to wonder as I sip my tea,
Is it a shark? No, it can't be.
Or maybe a hippo? Let's wait and see.
I soon knew when it rose up,
I accidentally dropped my cup.
It was a hippo, big and tall,
On its way to the nearest ball!

Emma Louise Patton (10)
St John The Baptist Primary School, Uddingston

THROUGH MY HORRID DOOR

Through my horrid door I can see
Evil skeletons crackling their bones
Shaking their heads
Popping
Up and down and all around
Off go the skeletons' heads

Trees swaying through the dark night
Branches like witches' fingers
Sharply poking me
Aarghh!
I scream louder and louder
Slamming shut my horrid door.

Matthew Mulholland (8)
St John The Baptist Primary School, Uddingston

THROUGH MY BEDROOM WINDOW

Through my bedroom window
I look up at the stars
I try to name planets and my favourite one is Mars
Aliens live on there you see
They travel through the night
They come down in their rocket ship
To give us all a fright

They land in fields and creep about
To see just where we stay
Their yellow skin and scary eyes
They have to hide by day
I like my alien friends a lot
When they come, I'm not alone
And after night-time comes the day
And they have to travel home.

Sean Brady (8)
St John The Baptist Primary School, Uddingston

THROUGH MY HAPPY DOOR

Through my happy door lies my make-believe land
A land so dazzling with beauty and colour
I call this my fairyland, full of fun and laughter

Elves dancing and singing till the sun goes down
Fairies twizzling and swizzling round the trees
Bunnies jumping and hopping around the town
Oh! What a wonderful land this is.

Mark McCaughley (8)
St John The Baptist Primary School, Uddingston

THROUGH MY MAGIC DOOR

Through my magic door I can see
The creatures of an ocean of trees,
Little monsters I can hardly see,
Deep holes in the ground covered in leaves.

The animals run along the scatter of leaves,
To get away from the huge *lion!*
Oh no, he's coming my way,
I'd better run.
He gets closer and closer, until,
At last he stops and picks me up in his paw,
Licks me and puts me in his mouth.
'Help!' I cry.

But then I have an idea, I rub my hair inside his tummy,
He spits me out - I hope I didn't taste yummy.

Kayleigh Bennett (8)
St John The Baptist Primary School, Uddingston

THROUGH MY MAGIC DOOR

Through my magic door I can see
A land of dragons
Playing a game of football on a lovely day
Dragons have green scales, like fish
I wish I was there

They can breathe out hot, boiling fire
Dragons have slimy skin
They have huge wings and can fly really high
I saw plain, pure-white eggs in a dragon's nest
I wish I was there.

Ryan Bain (8)
St John The Baptist Primary School, Uddingston

THE SAVAGE SEA

Crashing on the craggy rocks
Raging like the ravaging wind
Seagulls shirking, gashing splashes
Will the storm every rescind?

Lightning soaring fiercely by
Lighting up the ferocious sky
Fish dart, towering in the sea
Whatever will be, will be!

Boats bobbing on the lofty waves
Driftwood splashing by
Hacking furiously into hollow caves
A momentary sigh

Sky, a gloomy stretch of grey
Speckled with gusts of fleecy clouds
Fishermen of old have lost their way
Over untamed, serrated mounds

Hauling in the snaggy, barbed nets
Silver salmon slither away
'Tis all the hardy fishermen get
Waiting for hushed seas today

A flaxen light beams down from Heaven
Abate the time on wandering hour
Bands of gleaming colour, seven
The sea retreats its ebbing power

A silent calm falls on the peaceful tide
Still the water quiet and milk
The billowy waves creep down to hide
The sea, cradled as a sleeping child.

Natale Maccabe (10)
St John The Baptist Primary School, Uddingston

THROUGH MY MAGIC DOOR

Through my magic door I can see
Millions of funny little fairies
Singing lovely songs to each other
Being very happy

They are very cute
Sparkling wings, so bright and colourful
I wish I was there

Through my magic door I can see
Lots of tiny little people called fairies
Swinging on swings
Above a lovely, sparkling blue pond
They live
I wish I was there.

Lynsey Docherty (8)
St John The Baptist Primary School, Uddingston

THROUGH MY BEDROOM WINDOW

Through my bedroom window I can see
Cars rushing to work
Large vans dropping off things
The sun's light bursting through the smoky clouds
Children eating cold, buzzery ice cream
Birds whizzing through the warm air

Through my bedroom window I can hear
Birds whistling in the bushy trees
The wind's howling through the warm air.

Neil Morris (8)
St John The Baptist Primary School, Uddingston

THROUGH MY MAGIC DOOR

Through my magic door
I can see a land of dinosaurs
Wrestling and biting each other
Scratching and kicking
Roaring and screaming
Killing all their enemies
I wish I was there
I could help them win the war

I could fight and shout
Kick and scream
I could slay the dinosaurs
If I went through my magic door.

Liam McGarrell (8)
St John The Baptist Primary School, Uddingston

THROUGH MY MAGIC DOOR

Through my magic door I can see
Pond life creatures
Fast, cute and spotty newts swimming in a pond
Giant, warty, hopping toads hopping really fast
Small, blue dragonflies flying very slow
Tiny, little, green frogs eating loads of flies
Very small, black tadpoles are eating lots of weed
Lots and lots of slimy weed moving in the pond
A load of big, huge koi carp fish swimming through the weed
So much greeny, yucky pond water
And a lot of frogspawn
I wish I was a pond life creature.

Daniel Butler (8)
St John The Baptist Primary School, Uddingston

154

THROUGH THE MYSTERIOUS DOOR

Through my mysterious door there are dinosaurs
T-rex, brachiosaurus, spinosaurus and triceratops,
They all live in the dinosaur world
The brachiosaurus is very slow
And weighs more than a ton
T-rex is the enemy of them all
And so is the spinosaurus
When they both meet, they fight

Big and small
Long and short
I just can't choose which one I dread
I know I will choose a spinosaurus
I wish I was there.

Liam Hargan (8)
St John The Baptist Primary School, Uddingston

THROUGH MY MYSTERIOUS DOOR

Through my mysterious door
I can see a T-rex munching meat
He is never happy and he eats more and more
Till he is full from head to feet
His stomach is so full and sore
That he can no longer eat

In this land of giant reptiles
There are raptors running very fast
For miles and miles
On the green, green grass
And on the riverbank sits a snapping crocodile
Who lives today since the horrid past.

Paul Hewitt (8)
St John The Baptist Primary School, Uddingston

STAGE FRIGHT

This singer is very good,
She doesn't eat a lot of food.
She likes to draw, she likes to sing,
She has a certain lovely thing.

But, somehow she is scared,
Although she never cared.
When she went on the stage,
She ran off with rage.

A singer with stage fright,
Whoever saw such a sight?
She really made a lot of money,
She gave it all to her mummy.

Megan Coyle (10)
St John The Baptist Primary School, Uddingston

JOURNEYS

It was the 9th of July,
I was going on holiday to Portugal,
I was feeling nervous about the journey.
First I had to travel to London,
We went by car to the airport,
I was feeling nervous on the plane,
In London we had to wait at the airport,
Soon it was time to go on the plane to Portugal,
I was still feeling nervous,
I was happy when my journey was finished.

Sophie Walters (7)
St Kenneth's Primary School, East Kilbride

HONESTLY

Sittin' in ma bedroom,
thrown darts at ma wall,
leavin' clothes lyin' about,
puttin' on music to make you shout and bawl,
oh no, here comes Mum,
right about now, I need a chum,
honest, it wasnae me!

Comin' out of the bathroom,
leavin' a wet floor,
with the taps runnin'
and towels, what a bore!
Oh no, here comes Dad,
I've been really bad,
honest it wasnae me!

Lyin' on the couch,
watchin' Kerrang,
I chucked a pillow, it smashed a vase,
then broke Craig's bass,
now he's cryin',
time to start lyin',
honest, it wasnae me!

Sittin' in the kitchen,
eatin' ma dinner,
Craig, threw ma food at me,
it flew across the room like a bat,
I didn't put away the dishes
or even feed the fishes.
Help, here comes Mummy,
I've been really crummy,
honest, it wasnae me!

Andrew O'Brien (11)
St Kenneth's Primary School, East Kilbride

IT WASN'T ME

I put my wet bag dripping over the chair
I leave my shoes outside the door
I leave my daily rubbish on the table
It wasn't me.

My dirty clothes piled high like a pyramid
My room untidy with my make-up
Empty CD cases all over the place
It wasn't me.

I leave the TV left on
I take the cushions off the couch
Crumbs fall onto the floor
Please believe me, it wasn't me.

I put towels on the floor
Leave clothes all over the place
The floor's covered in water
It wasn't me.

Rachael Hall (11)
St Kenneth's Primary School, East Kilbride

THE MAGIC CAR

We have a magic car
That will whizz you all around,
To school, to shops, or swimming pool
Or even Glasgow Town.

If you tell the driver where
You would like to go,
You will find yourself right there
After you say, 'Let's go!'

The driver always knows the way,
About which I'm very glad,
Because you see the secret is
The chauffeur is my dad.

Emma Coll (10)
St Kenneth's Primary School, East Kilbride

A JOURNEY

In the middle of July
I awoke one day
The rain was not falling
And the sun was not far away

I looked at my clock
Five in the morning was the time
I got changed very quickly
I looked around my room not leaving a dime

I was going on holiday to Florida
I was going with my family, Mum and Dad
My mum told me it was time to go
To tell you the truth, I was quite glad

I sat in the car ready to go
As my dad closed the boot with a thump
My dad drove the car up the street
It seemed like forever but finally we stopped with a *bump*

We sat in the airport waiting for our flight to be called
I was hoping soon we'd be on our way
I checked the flight board and was pleased to see
Our flight was on time without a delay

Lynne Robertson (10)
St Kenneth's Primary School, East Kilbride

I'LL DO IT LATER

My games are on the floor,
I need to shut the door, so no one will see the mess.
Juice on the windowsill, I need to pretend I'm ill,
So I don't have to clean it up,
My bed's not made but
I'll do it later.

Papers on the couch,
Magazines all around,
Cans on the coffee table,
I'll do it later.

'Move your plate before it's too late,'
'Don't forget your milk,'
'I told you to stop watching The Hulk,'
I'll do it later.

My shoes are everywhere about,
Football boots and trainers scattered everywhere,
I thought I heard my mum shout, 'Tidy up!'
I'll do it later.

Mark Maguiness (11)
St Kenneth's Primary School, East Kilbride

TRAFFIC JAM

When the traffic is bad
Some people get mad
You are in your car
Hoping to travel far

Then the cars up ahead
Suddenly stop dead
You are stuck in a jam
Trying to keep calm

Now the traffic is moving
You're soon on your way
Your journey's nearly over
And it's taken you all day.

Peter Tinney (10)
St Kenneth's Primary School, East Kilbride

OOPS, I FORGOT

Spilling juice and leaving stains;
Like orange jelly.
The cosy couch; like a jumping
Bean bouncing.
Feet resting on the comfy couch,
Keeping warm.
Oops, I forgot!

Fighting with Susan; the great punch bag.
My messy room, like a big balloon.
Leaving clothes out, 'How messy of me.'
Oops, I forgot!

Leaving my phone charger in the hall,
'How thoughtful of me.'
Pile of minky messy clothes,
'Why can't they stay?'
Pyjamas piling outside my door,
'How else can I score?'
Oops, I forgot!

Lying lonely dishes; a nice collection.
Dirty towels on the table,
'What a nice display.'
Smelly, stinky fish; pooh, yuck.
Oops, I forgot!

Katie-Louise Rooney (10)
St Kenneth's Primary School, East Kilbride

DON'T BLAME IT ON ME!

School bag and shoes in a pile like a dump yard,
Dirty dishes lying in the sink,
Piled up like a mountain,
Hair accessories scattered like bits and bobs,
Don't *blame* it on me!

Jackets on the floor like a scattered rainbow,
Dishcloths on the couch like bits of litter,
Leaving the door open as if I was born in a park,
Don't *blame* it on me!

Overflowing cupboard like a camel's hump,
Dirty washing on the floor like a pile of muddled trash,
Cat food smelling of mouldy fish,
Don't *blame* it on me!

Dirty jackets like litter in a bin lorry,
Toys on the floor like a jumble sale,
Hair accessories like a clump of paint
Don't *blame* it on me!

Ashley McGregor (11)
St Kenneth's Primary School, East Kilbride

IN A MINUTE!

Clothes on the floor like a tower,
Duvet like a camel's hump on the bed,
Teddies scattered, magazines open, left alone,
'In a minute!'

Irn-Bru bottles on the worktop,
Cat food stuck to the grey tiles,
Dirty dishes left in the sink,
'In a minute!'

Eating food on the couch,
Walking on the floor with outdoor shoes,
Body lying on the couch,
'In a minute!'

Dirty plates piled on the floor,
Drawing paper scattered everywhere,
Messy bed with that just jumped-on look,
'In a minute!'

Megan Jane Campbell (11)
St Kenneth's Primary School, East Kilbride

I'VE FORGOTTEN

Passwords on the computer, as hard as hard can be,
Fighting in the PC room, bashing Damian's head on the table,
Bad language at Damian,
I've forgotten.

Fighting in my room, black eyes and bleeding teeth,
Not tidying my bed then my mum shouts,
Playing bad CDs and tapes,
I've forgotten.

Hiding my brother's CDs is fun,
Fighting is even better when my brother cries,
Making passwords on his computer so he can never get it started,
I've forgotten.

Scratching walls in the pool room with the cue,
Bad language, tut, tut, must shut up or I'm dead,
Mixing my dad's work folders up,
I've forgotten.

Kieran Marek Sanaghan (11)
St Kenneth's Primary School, East Kilbride

IT WASN'T ME

CDs on the floor,
Jumping on the bed,
Music on too loud,
No, it wasn't me.

Dishes not done,
'Please unpack the dishwasher,'
'No, not now,'
Juice on the floor,
No, it wasn't me.

Jumping on the couch,
Feet on the couch,
Couch broken,
No, it wasn't me.

Lift the wet bath mat up,
Toilet lid up,
Toilet not flushed,
No, it wasn't me.

Cameron Gosling (11)
St Kenneth's Primary School, East Kilbride

DON'T BLAME ME

Leaving dirty crumbs on the floor,
Not putting plates in the dishwasher,
Plus not doing the disgusting dishes,
Don't blame me.

Leaving the scratched CDs on the floor,
Jumping on the brand new couch,
Fighting with the feathered pillows,
Don't blame me.

Dropping the wet towels on the floor,
Leaving the overflowing bath on,
Not flushing the toilet,
Don't blame me.

Leaving a messy room behind you,
Not switching the electrical light off,
Not making your comfy bed,
Don't blame me.

Paul McGinlay (11)
St Kenneth's Primary School, East Kilbride

IT WASN'T ME

Door open, all are welcome,
Pillows on the floor, let's jump on them,
Empty bottles dropping off the window sill,
It wasn't me!

Dirty dishes full of grease,
Food on the floor like a mini dump,
Tap left gushing on twenty-four hours a day,
It wasn't me!

Toothpaste on floor like an extra large slug,
Blue eyeshadow on the sink, mascara on the towel,
Water exploded everywhere,
It wasn't me!

Dirty carpet caked in mud,
Sticky sweets on the floor,
Cuddly teddies chatting happily on my carpet
It wasn't me!

Susan Douglas (11)
St Kenneth's Primary School, East Kilbride

IT WAS LIKE THAT WHEN I GOT HERE!

Kitchen like a Picasso painting, it's not that bad,
Carpet full of crumbs and stains, could have been Dad?
Dishwasher's a state, dare to peer,
It was like that when I got here.

Stains on the new cream suite, not seen that before,
Eating on the carpet, Paul don't head for the door!
The TV's on, listen my dear,
It was like that when I got here.

Kerrang! magazines all over the floor, got lots of posters on the door,
Guitar and amp not put away, oh come on, I'll do it another day.
Cans and crisps and even some beer,
It was like that when I got here.

Towels, towels everywhere, for my hands and for my hair,
Cap on the toothpaste not put on right, from the teeth brushing
                              that was done last night.
The marks on the sink were made by a deer,
For the *last* time! It was like that when I got here!

Paul Cadwallender (11)
St Kenneth's Primary School, East Kilbride

IT WASN'T ME

Dirty dishes dumped in the sink,
Food flung on the floor, like a swamp,
Juice spilt on the table like a red sea,
It wasn't me.

Mud splattered on the bath,
Toothpaste oozing out of its tube,
Spilt bubble bath on the floor,
It wasn't me.

Clothes bundled on the floor like a mountain,
Room is like a bomb site,
CDs scattered everywhere,
It wasn't me.

Books lying on the table,
Jumping on the couch like a trampoline,
Broken vases, chipped plates,
It wasn't me.

Swathi Sethuraman (10)
St Kenneth's Primary School, East Kilbride

I Didn't Do It

Mmm, yum, making sandwiches, oops I've not washed my knife,
Nice shoes, is that a coat hanger? I've scattered my shoes
And jacket in the kitchen.
Come in, the door's open, oops the back door's open,
I didn't do it.

Oh that looks sore, what a wrestling match on the couch,
Is that where your bag goes? I left my bag behind the couch.
Ah, nice seat, that table is not a seat.
I didn't do it.

A towel rack on the floor, I left the towel on the bathroom floor,
A wardrobe in the bathroom, I've put my clothes on the floor.
That's disgusting, oh the toilet hasn't been flushed,
I didn't do it.

Tidy your room, I've not tidied my room,
My room is a crisp packet, I dropped crisps on the floor.
Nice bin, I left sweet wrappers on the floor,
I didn't do it.

Bobby McMonigle (11)
St Kenneth's Primary School, East Kilbride

I'LL DO IT IN A MINUTE!

The cream carpet's not hoovered
A mountain of clothes piled on the bed
TOTP mags lying on the floor
'I'll do it in a minute!'

Dirty dishes lying on the kitchen table
Milk spilled on dirty surfaces
Crumby biscuits left out
'I'll do it in a minute!'

A rainbow of towels lying on the floor
Sticky toothpaste on the window sill
Soapy water left in the sink
'I'll do it in a minute!'

Books down the side of chairs
The cups have been left on the table for a week
Oops, I left the door open
'I'll do it in a minute!'

Marianne Campbell (11)
St Kenneth's Primary School, East Kilbride

IT WASN'T ME

Muddy shoes all over the hall,
Annoying my sister when she comes through the door,
Brand new carpet all covered in mud,
It wasn't me!

A 4ft high heap of clothes,
CDs on the floor like a carpet,
A flood of comics coming out the door,
It wasn't me!

A dump of dirty dishes,
A wave of overflowing rubbish,
Fridge door left lying open,
It wasn't me!

Racket from the TV left on,
Broken springs in the couch,
Glass smashed because of lights smashed,
It wasn't me!

Chris Kenny (11)
St Kenneth's Primary School, East Kilbride

JOURNEYS

I have had seven different teachers,
But I've only had the same one twice.
That was when we were in Primary 1 and 2,
When we were just like little mice.

Then I was in Primary 3,
I was a very bad child so the teacher was always after me.
Then it got harder because I was in Primary 4
And that was a real bore.

Then I was in Primary 5
And that was when I came alive.

Then I was in Primary 6
And that was when I was breaking sticks.

Then I was in Primary 7
And that is like being in Heaven.

Michelle Dowling (11)
St Kenneth's Primary School, East Kilbride

A JOURNEY IN THE METAL BIRD

Stepping up into the metal bird's belly
My hungry tummy jumps and my legs feel like jelly
The passengers are like worms
For the birds to eat
Her tasty morning breakfast
As I take my seat
I feel a little nervous but excited too
Just like a small bird the first time it flew
The bird jumps high and we leap into the air
Below there are roads and rivers
Like a long strand of hair
I feel powerful and strong up here in the cloud
And I imagine our lady in her beautiful blue shroud
It is nice to dream when you are high up here
With no traffic and noise or horns in your ears
The captain says coming down now from 33,000 feet
Fasten your belts and stay in your seats
And as my aeroplane journey comes to an end
I say thank you to the metal bird, my new best friend.

Nathan Ross (9)
St Kenneth's Primary School, East Kilbride

MY JOURNEY

It was a scorching day
It was the middle of May
Running up to the train
Oh please I hope it doesn't rain

On the train it is too hot
Everyone is moaning a lot
It's so busy and loud
Because of the crowd

Going along I see cities and towns
We go over a mountain, I cannot look down
How long will this journey be?
I just can't wait to be by the sea

Oh, now I can see the water
Can it get any hotter?
Here on the beach, it's so great
I knew it was definitely worth the wait.

Conor Mullan (9)
St Kenneth's Primary School, East Kilbride

WELL, SORRY

My clothes were on the floor and I said, 'No more.'
My CDs out of their cases, I put them away just in case,
My muddy shoes on the floor, I ran away and said, 'No more.'
Well, except from 'Well, sorry! It wasn't my fault.'

My towel on the floor, I again said, 'No more.'
My bath tub mucky and the rubber ducky said, 'Mucky.'
The perfume stunk and so did I. I said, 'Well, sorry.'

On the living room seat that's where I eat my meat,
The TV's dusty, don't look at me.
Ornaments barely standing up,
The place was like a big fat dump.
Well I'm sorry, it wasn't just me.

I have a spare room, it's not got a broom,
That's too bad, I'll blame it on Dad,
The light gave me a fright because it was so bright,
Well, sorry!

James Duddy (11)
St Kenneth's Primary School, East Kilbride

IT WASN'T ME

My room
CDs and videos scattered around in the colour of a rainbow
And as you get to the bottom of the rainbow
There's two blue cups
It wasn't me

The living room
Big, blue designer marks on the brand new cream sofa
The marks came off my bag
Leave the door open so everyone can come in and see
It wasn't me

The kitchen
Crumbs, sparkling fairy dust all over the floor
My brother comes in, we start to fight
I put the TV on to watch my best programme
Oops, I didn't turn it off
It wasn't me.

The spare room
Paper on the ground, leaving things around
Pencils, pens lying on the desk
It wasn't me.

Lauren Lafferty (11)
St Kenneth's Primary School, East Kilbride

JOURNEYS

Summer holidays
Today's the day we go away
Mum and Dad, sister and me

It's a rainy day
We might get delayed
Mum and Dad, sister and me

We board the plane
We're on our way
Mum and Dad, sister and me

We land in Ibiza
We'll play all day
Mum and Dad, sister and me.

James Wallace (8)
St Kenneth's Primary School, East Kilbride

AEROPLANES

A large white painted body,
E ngines and two wings,
R un aboard and experience some new and exciting things!
O n it you will travel a thousand miles or more,
P lease check out the window,
L ook through for views galore
A nd now we're getting faster,
N ext we leave the ground,
E veryone can hear the
S creeching engine sounds!

A nd now the buildings look smaller,
N ow the cars look minute,
D on't stop climbing higher.

F or now we're following the air route,
L ook! We're going through the clouds,
I t's so misty, we can't see!
G et something from the trolley.
H ey! Nothing's for free!
T rue it is, we're landing! The journey - it is through!
But don't you look so glum now! There is still the holiday too!

Joanna Maphin (11)
St Kenneth's Primary School, East Kilbride

JOURNEYS

It was the summer holidays,
I was going to Ireland,
Into the car I climbed,
Off we set on our journey.
Finally we arrived at the boat station,
Went up to the top deck.
But when the boat got started,
I didn't feel so great.
Hurry! Get me a sick bag!
I think I might need to use it.

At long last we got off the boat,
We begin to drive again.
Will this journey ever end?
We stop off at a café,
For a drink and a bite to eat.
Will I be sick?
Then we set off again,
I soon fall asleep,
I am rudely awakened,
Car doors are banging . . .
It's 1am in the morning,
Our journey has ended.

Fiona Cunning (9)
St Kenneth's Primary School, East Kilbride

JOURNEY TO THE BEACH

In summer I like to fly
In an aeroplane high in the sky,
Menorca, Majorca, Turkey, Spain,
Oh, I could go there again and again.

I like to travel far and far,
When we go out in our car.
The sun may shine, the rain may pour,
We all enjoy the seashore.

Conor Sullivan (8)
St Kenneth's Primary School, East Kilbride

A JOURNEY

J   ust as we were about to go
O   ur train raced away
U   nder the tunnels
R   aced through the country
N   ot going very slow
E   veryone was angry
Y   et we caught another one.

Sinead Toner (8)
St Kenneth's Primary School, East Kilbride

JOURNEY

Cars rushing,
Wind whooshing,
Trees dancing,
Dogs walking,
Happy, excited,
A good day at school.

Kerry Harkin (6)
St Kenneth's Primary School, East Kilbride

JOURNEY

July this year
Holiday time again
The cases were packed
Off we went!
Journey started

A car trip to Manchester
Plane delayed four hours
Fed-up waiting
Aboard at last
Plane journey started

Long way to go
Dozed on the way
Plane landed
America!
Journey over.

Ryan Doran (8)
St Kenneth's Primary School, East Kilbride

IT WASN'T ME

Plates smashed, china shattered
Vases bashed, chips without fish
Dirty boots, one inch mud
It wasn't me

Soaking coat, dripping with mud
Fell in a moat, absolutely drenched
Dirty hands, mucky mess
It wasn't me

Untidy room, crisp packets and crumbs
Ghetto blasters boom, full volume
Bad manners, no knife or fork
It wasn't me

Things lying around, juice spills
Troubles bound, slamming the door
Couch busted, springs popping up
It wasn't me.

Robert O'Connell (11)
St Kenneth's Primary School, East Kilbride

JOURNEYS

It was summer,
I was going on my holidays,
I was excited.
Dad drove to the bus station,
Our journey had started.

We took the bus to the airport,
We went on the plane,
I was excited.
The plane landed after three hours,
Our journey was nearly over.

We took another bus to the pier,
We went on a boat,
I was still excited.
We reached the island,
Then we walked to our holiday home,
Our journey was over.

Gina Colley (8)
St Kenneth's Primary School, East Kilbride

DIRTY CRIMES

I left handprints on the bathroom wall,
I told a tale so very tall,
Of 'I didn't do it' and 'it wasn't me'
And how I didn't spill the tea,
Of untidy rooms and slamming the door
And rock CDs left on the floor.
I turned the music up to full volume,
As the player exploded with a sonic boom!
Really, I am a problem child,
As I am as wild as wild.
Who broke the table and bust the settee?
Everybody's blaming me.
Muddy shoes left on the floor
And banana skins and apple cores,
I left chess pieces lying around
And left my clothes all in a mound,
On the TV I dropped a hammer,
Which is why I'm in the slammer!

Andrew Johnstone (11)
St Kenneth's Primary School, East Kilbride

WALKING TO SCHOOL

We like coming to school,
We can see the busy road,
We can hear the noise of the cars,
We can smell the fresh air,
We can hear the children in the playground,
They are laughing and playing,
Walking to school is fun.

Room 4
St Kenneth's Primary School, East Kilbride

IN A MINUTE

Wrappers left on the table like a dump
Door left open for everyone
PC disks left out of cases
In a minute!

Eating all the biscuits
Leaving the drawers wide open
Dirty dishes piled up like the Eiffel Tower
In a minute!

Shoes caked with mud lying in the hall
Messy shoe cupboard with shoes piled high
Coat on the floor too
In a minute!

Not tidying my room
Leaving the dirty washing scattered everywhere
Lights left on like a Christmas tree too
In a minute!

Suzanne Page (11)
St Kenneth's Primary School, East Kilbride

JOURNEYS

When I travel, I go very far
Cycling on my bike or in my car
When I went on the boat to Ireland
I got very tired
There are many ways to travel
You can use your imagination or your education
Whether it's a bus, car or plane
There's no reason to complain.

Alyson Canning (8)
St Kenneth's Primary School, East Kilbride

JOURNEYS

It's the summer holiday,
It's the 23rd of July,
I'm off to Oasis,
It is very exciting.
On the journey it's a steady ride,
I draw and write and read,
The fun is about to begin.

We took a picnic,
Lots of food - sandwiches, crisps and sweets,
After an hour we stopped to eat,
We began to eat our lunches.
We set off again,
But in no time at all we're there,
The fun is about to begin.

Nicola Robson (8)
St Kenneth's Primary School, East Kilbride

JOURNEYS

Holidays!
Where will I go?
What will I travel on?
So much to choose!
Planes! Trains! Cars! Boats!
A cruise?
A big, fancy boat!
All kinds of things to do.
I think I'll set sail.

Megan McKenna (8)
St Kenneth's Primary School, East Kilbride

JOURNEYS

Seven o'clock in the morning
A lovely summer's day in July
A-camping we were going!

All was packed
Off we set
A-camping we were going!

Games and comics kept us busy
Picnic lunch on the way
A-camping we were going!

Reached the campsite
Put up tent
A-camping all the way!

Daniel Kelly (8)
St Kenneth's Primary School, East Kilbride

JOURNEYS

We were in a Land Rover,
Going to Dover.
When we got there I was very merry,
We loaded the car onto the ferry.
I watched the waves trickling by,
We're almost there and my spirit is high.
The ferry came to a stop in Calais,
We went in a car to our chalet.

Charlotte-Marie Young (9)
St Kenneth's Primary School, East Kilbride

JOURNEYS

We're going on holiday today
Flying and buying, coming our way
We're going on a plane
All the way to Spain

Now it's time to go
In the car we go
Stop at the airport
Get on the plane
For the journey to Spain

We're in the air in no time at all
I get some peanuts
'We're nearly there' the pilot calls
I shout, 'Hip hip hooray, we're nearly in Spain,'

The pilot finally lands the plane
We are now in Spain
And our long journey is finally over.

Christopher Doherty (9)
St Kenneth's Primary School, East Kilbride

MAGIC JOURNEYS

Magic journeys are fun, you can see magic animals,
Unicorns, magic birds, magic owls and magic dragons.
You can see magic round the corner,
When you jump in it, you go on a magic travelling dream.

Ruairidh Sawers (7)
St Kenneth's Primary School, East Kilbride

JOURNEYS

We're going on a vacation,
Buses, boats or planes?
So many ways to travel!
Which one will take me on my holiday?
I feel so excited.
It's so nerve crackling.
I can't take it any longer.
Oh! Why can't someone tell me what we're going on?
I don't have to wait any longer.
I hope we're not walking!
I hope we go in a car.
We go out the door and into the car.
We're heading to the airport.
I am so happy.
I'm going on a plane.
Soon the airport is in sight.
Lots of planes.
Which one am I going on?
I just don't know.
My dad's out the car.
So we head into the airport.
I can't believe my eyes,
There is such a huge queue.
Soon it is time to go onto the plane,
The plane is so cool.
I sit beside the window waving to the people below.
My journey has started.

Jennifer Reid (9)
St Kenneth's Primary School, East Kilbride

JOURNEYS

I went on a plane to Mallorca,
It was a lovely day in July,
I thought my oh my, I'm going to Mallorca,
It's going to be great, I can't wait,
When we came back we were sad,
No one glad,
So after the summer holidays I went back to school,
Believe me, that wasn't cool,
Doing lots of work and no fun
And plus, there is no sun,
Now winter is here and it's cold
And I wish that I was back in Mallorca,
In the sun and having lots of fun.

Kathleen McCartney (11)
St Kenneth's Primary School, East Kilbride

JOURNEYS

It's the summer holidays,
Sitting in the car.
Wonder where we're going,
Nicola's sitting beside me,
I am getting excited.
The road is bumpy,
I feel sick,
Mum puts the radio on,
I feel better,
We're going to England,
I feel happy.

Katrina McAinsh (9)
St Kenneth's Primary School, East Kilbride

MY FAVOURITE JOURNEY

Waking up one morning
I felt very glad
I was going on a journey
With Neil, Chris. Mum and Dad

We got our things together
And loaded up the car
We set off on our way
'Cause we were going far

Finally we arrived
We were driving for five hours
I was very excited
We'd arrived at Alton Towers.

Jasmine Kenny (10)
St Kenneth's Primary School, East Kilbride

MY JOURNEY

Today's the day we go on holiday,
We got in the car and started our long journey to the airport.
When we got to the airport we went to check-in
And then went to board the plane.
But when we sat down the captain announced that the flight would be
Delayed for half an hour, so we just sat and waited.
When the flight finally took off, we got our dinner
And then had to wait another hour until we got there.
When we got there we got a bus to our hotel
And our auntie showed us to our room.
Before we unpacked we decided we would go for a good night's sleep
After our long journey.

John McLaren (8)
St Kenneth's Primary School, East Kilbride

MY JOURNEY TO THE ZOO

On my journey to the zoo,
I saw the leaves falling off their trees,
Then I wondered what would it be like?
Will the lions bite or will the kangaroo fight?
Now I'm coming up to the bridge
And my mum shouts back, 'Hold on tight.'
My dad said, 'Don't worry, I won't pick a fight.'
Now we're over that scary bridge,
I can sit back and go to sleep.
I dreamt of what it would be like,
Five minutes later my mum shouted, 'Right.'
I opened my eyes, we were finally there,
I jumped out the car
And ran straight to the bear.

Maddie McCartney (9)
St Kenneth's Primary School, East Kilbride

JOURNEYS

I was with you when you were born, *pop!*
I was with you when you said your first words, *Mama.*
I was with you when you took your first steps.
I was with you when you fell and cut your knee.
I was with you when you learnt to ride your bike.
I was with you when you met your crush.
I was with you when you first kissed him.
I will be with you when you pass your driving test.
I will be with you when you get married
And I will definitely be with you through your other journeys.

Rosa Neville (11)
St Kenneth's Primary School, East Kilbride

JOURNEYS

You can travel on a plane or even on a train,
There are many ways of travelling around the world.
The plane flies high in the sky,
Whilst a car zooming by in the street going,
Beep, beep, beep!
Trains on the tracks,
A-chug-a-tee chug,
Everything's going very fast!

There are things in the sky and things down below,
But they are all journeying around the world.
Take a slow boat to China or try a world cruise,
There are so many ways to travel,
Which one would you choose?

Katie Lee (11)
St Kenneth's Primary School, East Kilbride

I WENT ON A JOURNEY

Once an old man set off on a journey,
All his friends went too.
He didn't stop or waste his time
Or sit down or frown.
His feet kept on the ground.
I met the old man,
I joined him and set off too.
I waved goodbye and my mum began to cry,
But soon it passed away,
Until Monday when I came back,
With a big, black sack full of things
I'd learned on my journey.

Chelsea Tizard (7)
St Kenneth's Primary School, East Kilbride

THE ZOO

I went on a journey to the zoo,
It was hot, very, very hot.
It was fun.
Then I went over to see the lion,
It roared at me.
I was scared.
Then I said, 'I don't want to see that again.'
Then I went to see the hippo,
It went under the water and when it came out again,
It squirted water at me.
I was wet, very, very wet.
Then I went to see the dolphin show,
It was good, very, very good.
But it was getting late, very, very late,
Then I went home.
Then I said, 'Home sweet home.'

Louise O'Donnell (8)
St Kenneth's Primary School, East Kilbride

THE PYRAMIDS OF EGYPT

Walking in the pyramids is scary,
There's no lights, so it's hard to find the way,
I can feel unusual carvings on the wall,
Walking on the sand burns,
It is very hot,
There's nothing to be heard, except from people's feet,
I'm looking for a mummy's tomb
And suddenly, *bang.*

Jill McNee (9)
St Kenneth's Primary School, East Kilbride

HIDDEN TREASURES

H idden treasures in the deep,
I   n a chest all gleaming gold,
D anger is to seek this chest,
D anger is to try and open,
E ven if you are strong and brave,
N ever shall you get this chest.

T reasures I will find today,
R eal treasure.
E ven if it drives me to my grave,
A ll I wish to see is treasure,
S econds, minutes, hours or days,
U sing radar I shall find
R eal treasure,
E verlasting riches I will have,
S pending all my money.

Mhari Bryce (11)
St Mary's Primary School, Larkhall

AUTUMN

All the leaves are gold and brown,
Beautiful until they fall to the ground,
Then the wind twirls them round and round.

Gather in a heap, cosy together,
Fun to tread on in gloomy weather,
Welly boots will now be worn,
In puddles caused
By an autumn storm.

Jenna Louise Walker (8)
St Mary's Primary School, Larkhall

HIDDEN TREASURE

In my messy room playing my PlayStation,
Mum calls on me, 'Kevin, come downstairs
Come and eat your dinner.'
But as I went, something strange happened,
Aaarrggh! A trapdoor opened
And I fell down where I did not know.
My heart was pounding as I walked around,
Trying to find my way out,
When in the corner, I see a light,
Something there is shining bright.
It cannot be - it's amazing,
What comes into sight.
It's gold - gold bricks lying in a stack.
I take the gold bricks into my room,
Ready to hide them there,
When I remember my mother had my dinner ready,
Down the stair.
So I tiptoe out to my backyard
To hide the gold out there,
I could build a wall round and round,
So no one finds it there,
But I hear my mother call and I realise with a fright,
That I had had a lovely dream
And there is not a gold bar in sight.

Kevin Craigens (9)
St Mary's Primary School, Larkhall

MY CAT, FELIX

Felix has lovely long hair,
that reaches down to the ground,
but when he is silly
he runs round and round.

His eyes are hazel, his nose is pink
and when he watches television
he likes to watch *Monsters Inc*,
I love him a lot.

Jennifer McCrum (8)
St Mary's Primary School, Larkhall

HIDDEN TREASURE

I moved into the sea,
In my rusty submarine,
The sea was a dark blue,
The seaweed a bright green.

Underwater the submarine went,
Fifty metres the dial did measure,
But then I saw something shining brightly,
Under the water I had found some hidden treasure.

The little claws picked up the treasure,
Then stored it in the back,
I moved towards the box very shocked
And gave the padlock a great whack.

Inside the box lay lots of treasure,
Worth millions and millions of pounds,
There were watches, rings, gold and diamonds
And strange objects, sharp and round.

I floated back up the surface,
Being out the water gave me great pleasure,
It was a very successful ride,
Since I had found some hidden treasure.

Stephen Tracey (11)
St Mary's Primary School, Larkhall

HIDDEN TREASURES

Two men on a quest,
On a quest to find a chest,
A chest full of gold
And other treasures untold.

As they looked about,
Passing catfish and trout,
They kept on listening,
Until they saw glistening.

They have finished their quest,
They have found the chest,
The chest full of gold
And other treasures untold.

When they opened the chest,
They found that the quest
Was no more than a silly
Waste of time.

Michael Bent (11)
St Mary's Primary School, Larkhall

HIDDEN TREASURES

In a room of very, very dark things
Lies a darkened floorboard,
Made of wood with cracks and rats,
With something gold under the board.

The boy went into the attic,
It looked like a black painted room,
He stepped on a blue floorboard,
Now he was coming to his doom.

The boy was now pleading for his life,
He was sweating, in tears,
A rat made him slip from the floorboards,
Now this was the worst of his fears.

Ahhh! Cling, cling,
The boy woke up full of life,
In a room that was so cold,
He felt something hard on his back,
It was a ton of *gold!*

Greg Hamilton (10)
St Mary's Primary School, Larkhall

HIDDEN TREASURES

Here I go in the sea
Where I can barely breathe
I look at fish looking at me
I see the bright yellow box
Shining like the sun

I quickly swim over
To the blinding, shining box
Then I quickly open it
The brightness was all so beautiful
And the diamond necklaces and watches would probably
Be worth over a million pounds
Suddenly my oxygen started to get low
And I knew I had to go
I went to the top of the water
And I thought to myself -
I wonder if that will still be there when I am older?

Michael Tracey
St Mary's Primary School, Larkhall

HIDDEN TREASURES

I jump into my submarine
Ready to explore
Down, down, down we go
Deeper than before.

Oh look, there's a shark,
Oh look, there's a fish,
Oh look, there's an oyster,
In its pearly dish.

I feel we're getting closer,
I feel we're getting near,
I feel we're sinking down, down, down,
I know I have no fear.

Suddenly I spot it,
A pirate's treasure chest,
My hands shaking, I turn the lock
And wow! Out poured gold and jewels.

Susanne Martin (10)
St Mary's Primary School, Larkhall

HIDDEN TREASURES

I heard about hidden treasures,
Treasures under the sand,
Treasures that sound so grand.

I saw the hidden treasures,
They were so grand,
There were rings and things.

I took the treasures home,
I hid them in my room,
My sister shouted, 'Hidden treasures.'

The next day I was dead,
My mum had the hidden treasures,
'Oh no, I'm doomed!' I screamed.

Siobhan Keeney (10)
St Mary's Primary School, Larkhall

HIDDEN TREASURES

My treasure can be a monster,
But deep down they are really nice,
They like to pretend to be a famous dancer or footballer,
Their favourite dinner is macaroni rice.

I can tell them a deep, dark secret,
That I don't tell anyone else
And know that they will keep it
From humans, brownies and elves.

I tell them fairytale stories
About witches, fairies and wretched beasts
And not about the Labour Party or the Tories,
Who rule the towns and cities.

By now you must know or maybe you guessed,
How much I love my cousins so,
They're my hidden treasure,
The most wonderful sight to behold.

Samantha McMurray (9)
St Mary's Primary School, Larkhall

HIDDEN TREASURES

'Ahoy me mates
And ship ahoy.'
Set sail for the Mediterranean Sea,
To an island just for me,
Where hidden treasure is unknown,
Until now
And me, the captain,
Strong and tall, will dig,
Until it's found.
'X' marks the spot
On my treasure map.
We land on the island of Choris,
I dig until *bang! Clank!*
The shovel hits something hard,
I've found it, I've found it,
The treasures of my dream.

Robyn Young (10)
St Mary's Primary School, Larkhall

HIDDEN TREASURES

Down at the bottom of the ocean,
Deep below the surface of the sea,
I see lots of scary fish and sharks
And they're all looking straight at me.

As we reach the old abandoned ship,
Our sub begins to flip
Because a whale is swimming past
And he's going quite fast,
He must be hungry because he's licking his lips.

Dean McGough (10)
St Mary's Primary School, Larkhall

HIDDEN TREASURES

My cousin and me
Were climbing a tree,
Down at the bottom of the garden.

We could see the river
That had been there forever
And it shone like a lot of sapphires.

We went to see what the glow could be
And it was a small, green gem,
We thought it was yellow,
But then mellow yellow.

We looked some more
And found tons more,
There was enough to fill our pockets.

This was some hidden treasure,
It sure was a pleasure
To find such a treasure.

David Hillhouse (10)
St Mary's Primary School, Larkhall

MY HAMSTER

My hamster jumps about crazy
I know she is not lazy
I love to see her in her ball
Rolling, rolling in the hall
But even when she bites me
I still love her a lot.

Philip Martin (8)
St Mary's Primary School, Larkhall

HIDDEN TREASURES

Deep underwater there is a hidden treasure
The pirates hid it from me
I went down and down but didn't see anything
Then I saw an old ship below me
I went down to the ship and went into it
I searched the whole ship and didn't find anything
Then I saw a shining light, I went over to it
It was the hidden treasure
I wonder what is in it?
I took the treasure up to shore
Then I opened the hidden treasure chest
It was full of gold and money
I took the treasure home
I put the treasure in a cupboard.

Steven McMurray (11)
St Mary's Primary School, Larkhall

MY DOG

He has long, floppy ears
And a short, waggy tail
He runs around crazy
When he is excited

I always play ball with him
And he always jumps upon me
Shhh, he's asleep
That will be it for today.

Nicole McLaughlin (8)
St Mary's Primary School, Larkhall

THE BIG GAME

It was a Barca and Real game,
A big old firm,
I had waited for this,
The whole football term.

Real had kick-off,
They went up with the ball,
But they were too skinny,
For that Barca defensive wall.

The game was fast and furious,
It was getting a bit sick,
There was such a dirty tackle by Figo,
I thought he'd go to Auld Nick.

At last, the ref blew the final whistle,
It was boring, so they say,
It ended a rubbish 0-0,
Some football game, eh?

Niall Brown (8)
St Mary's Primary School, Larkhall

MY DOG, FONZ

My dog, Fonz has floppy ears,
When he doesn't get any food,
Suddenly he is in tears,
I let him play with me always.

My dog loves to go for walks
And chase people everywhere.

Keith Barnes (8)
St Mary's Primary School, Larkhall

HIDDEN TREASURES

In a chest far down beneath
Hidden treasures glimmering and shining,
Many try to find it
And are never seen again

Down at the bottom of the deep blue sea
Where the biggest creatures lurk
This priceless treasure is hidden
Behind a rock, beneath the sand

So many places it could be
Under that blue, shimmering sea
Finding it would leave you
Swimming in riches forever more.

Laura McCallion (11)
St Mary's Primary School, Larkhall

MY PUPPY

My puppy is called Patch,
He always likes to scratch.
My mum always gives him a smack,
But I give him a snack.

He always likes to run
And have lots of fun.
He always jumps upon me
And scratches me on the knee.
I still love him.

Carla McMurray (8)
St Mary's Primary School, Larkhall

HIDDEN TREASURES

Hidden treasures, underwater,
I wonder what I'll find?
An octopus with eight arms,
Asking, 'What's the time?'

Hidden treasures, underwater,
I wonder what I'll find?
A shark with lots of teeth,
Says, 'It's dinner time!'

Hidden treasures, underwater,
I wonder what I'll find?
A great big chest full of money,
I wonder if there's chocolate inside?

Sion McGeechan (11)
St Mary's Primary School, Larkhall

HIDDEN TREASURE

One summer's morning I woke up
And there I saw a note,
It said, 'Go in the den
And wait for my friend
And she will give you a note.'
Then she came
It said, 'Go to the garden gates.'
There was a white piece of paper there
It said, 'Go to the park.'
So I went to the park
And there I saw my hidden treasure
It was sweets.

Rachel Hardie (10)
St Mary's Primary School, Larkhall

MY TREASURE

I found a secret room and walked through the door,
I found myself inside a maze that twizzled and turned,
I saw a little signpost marked a secret garden,
This must be a joke I thought,
But just kept on walking.
I heard a little chirping noise,
So I followed that sound,
Soon I came to a cage and quickly looked around,
Small birds, coloured brown, white, red and grey
Fluttered round that cage.
Gently I picked it up and carried it back the way I'd come,
Through that maze and secret door until I was safely home,
I kept my birds - safe inside my room,
My very special treasure, for me alone.

Kayleigh Douglas (9)
St Mary's Primary School, Larkhall

HIDDEN TREASURE

My treasure is a good thing for me
It's very lucky for me
It's in a place that only I know
It is by now that you should know
It is my good luck charm
A coin I got at school one day
My brother was going to pay me money
To get it that day
But I said, 'No'
So I still have it today
Hidden away.

David Newall (9)
St Mary's Primary School, Larkhall

MY HIDDEN TREASURE

I'm on an exotic island,
I have lost my sweetheart mum,
I must go and look for her
Or my tum will rum and rum.

I am shaking all around,
But I dare not stop to think,
Or I'll starve and starve
And sleep all day and night.

I wandered all around,
But I could not find my mum,
But then I saw this tall rectangle,
Perhaps it's my mum?

But then when I got closer,
It did not look like my mum,
But then I realised it was a transporter,
I could use that to find my mum!

Jennifer Little (9)
St Mary's Primary School, Larkhall

MY HIDDEN TREASURES

Underneath my bed I hide my secret treasure
It is wrapped in bluey-purply paper
If you pull the paper
Then put it on your tongue
You taste that lovely chocolate taste
And then it's all gone!

Stuart Deadman (9)
St Mary's Primary School, Larkhall

HIDDEN TREASURES

Under my bed, big and red
A hidden treasure all of my own,
It's all my favourite football colours.
My friend came down, he spotted the bag
And suddenly he heard a big, loud bang,
The water was whishing and slopping about,
The bag was flying in the air,
That's the day I'll never forget,
The day Kevin found my hidden treasure lying there.
If you want to know what my treasure was,
I'll have to tell you because you'll never know,
Because my treasure was water balloons,
That have gone - *pop, bang!*
Way to go!

Jordan Fleming (9)
St Mary's Primary School, Larkhall

MY HIDDEN TREASURE FROM MY HEART

Step through the door and guess what you'll see?
It will be a surprise just for you and me
Two big, dark eyes and a long, furry tail
Hidden outside, sheltered from rain and hail
In a pretty little house just made for one
It is my dog called Gemma
Who is really good fun
I take her for walks which she loves to do
With her doggy friends she loves to play
But enjoys coming home with me every day.

Nicola McGuire (9)
St Mary's Primary School, Larkhall

MY HIDDEN TREASURES

On Saturday morning the sun was shining,
So down the path I went skipping,
I heard a noise from the green bush in the garden,
There was a little brown puppy,
Alone and probably starving.
Cold and shivering,
I'll bring her out of the bush
And give her some milk and a blanket,
I'll get something to sit her in,
If I'm lucky maybe a basket.
I'll tell Mum and Dad I've found a puppy,
Maybe they will help me find the owner,
If we're lucky,
If we can't find her owner,
We'll take good care of her,
Like she was my hidden treasure.

Siobhan McGuigan (9)
St Mary's Primary School, Larkhall

SOMETHING PRECIOUS

In a very dark place lies my hidden treasure,
All damp and musty, but very precious,
Under some boxes, open a little flap
And soon you will find my hidden treasure.

Oh! What could it be, but some golden pennies in a golden box,
This is my hidden treasure,
But nobody must know because if anyone finds it,
It will disappear and go.

Nadia Crolla (9)
St Mary's Primary School, Larkhall

HIDDEN TREASURE

Down at the bottom of the garden
I found a treasure map
I started to follow it with my friend, Matt
We swung over rivers
We climbed over trees
We rolled under barbed wire
By this time we were dirty
By this time it was dark
I saw a red cross
We both started digging
And found a big, big chest
We both opened it and looked in
It was full of chocolate coins
We stuffed our faces
It was divine.

Mark McCluskey (10)
St Mary's Primary School, Larkhall

MY FAMILY

Deep in my secret drawer,
Lies something dear to me,
A picture with a frame,
It's of three people close to me.

Really, it's not a secret,
They live in my house,
Have you guessed yet?
My hidden treasure is my family.

Andrew Laird (9)
St Mary's Primary School, Larkhall

HIDDEN TREASURES

Away up there,
Where nobody goes,
There's a confidential secret,
That nobody knows.

Space is what I'm saying,
Just a big, dark-blue sky,
I will tell you something,
So you'll never pass it by.

Up there in the darkness,
Something never seen before,
Better than your wildest dreams,
Of gold and gold galore.

Okay, by now you should have guessed,
It makes you very fat,
Fine, I'll tell you anyway,
It's lovely brown chocolate!

Christopher Burns (11)
St Mary's Primary School, Larkhall

MY HIDDEN TREASURE

Hidden deep in my secret drawer lies my treasure,
It's very, very special to me,
As you would know if you had to see,
It sparkles and glimmers in the light,
It's truly amazing, colourful and bright,
Have you guessed it?
That's right! It's a diamond necklace,
What a beautiful sight.

Melissa Quinn (9)
St Mary's Primary School, Larkhall